A WOMAN OF

Purpose

Finding Self and　Making a Difference

Valarie F. Thomas

WESTBOW
PRESS®
A DIVISION OF THOMAS NELSON
& ZONDERVAN

WestBow Press books may be ordered through booksellers or by contacting:

WestBow Press
A Division of Thomas Nelson & Zondervan
1663 Liberty Drive
Bloomington, IN 47403
www.westbowpress.com
1 (866) 928-1240

Because of the dynamic nature of the Internet, any web addresses or links contained in this book may have changed since publication and may no longer be valid. The views expressed in this work are solely those of the author and do not necessarily reflect the views of the publisher, and the publisher hereby disclaims any responsibility for them.

Any people depicted in stock imagery provided by Getty Images are models, and such images are being used for illustrative purposes only. Certain stock imagery © Getty Images.

Unless otherwise indicated, all Scripture is taken from the King James Version of the Bible.

Scripture quotations marked (NIV) are taken from the Holy Bible, New International Version®, NIV®. Copyright © 1973, 1978, 1984, 2011 by Biblica, Inc.™ Used by permission of Zondervan. All rights reserved worldwide. www.zondervan.comThe "NIV" and "New International Version" are trademarks registered in the United States Patent and Trademark Office by Biblica, Inc.™

ISBN: 978-1-9736-9056-6 (sc)
ISBN: 978-1-9736-9057-3 (hc)
ISBN: 978-1-9736-9055-9 (e)

Library of Congress Control Number: 2020907333

Print information available on the last page.

WestBow Press rev. date: 05/11/2020

CONTENTS

DEDICATION

Although many people have shaped my life, I would like to dedicate this book to my mom, who has always had my back. When I was moving through life during my struggles, her words to me were, "Just keep going and one day you will step out on dry land." She is truly an inspiration and an amazing woman of God. She has taught me so much about staying in the fight of life and trusting God to bring me through while developing a Godly character that has surely brought me to this point.

ACKNOWLEDGMENTS

I am forever grateful for the challenges I have faced in life and the people God has placed in my path. Those people—past, present, and future—have shaped and will shape my course. I am also grateful for the family God has given me in the arrangement of wonderful, loving Christian parents and siblings. My parents taught me the meaning of loving God and loving others. I am now blessed to have a family of my own and have made every effort to pass along the teachings of my parents in hopes that my children will walk in complete submission to the Word of God, and that His Word will guide every decision they make in life. I am most thankful for my amazing spouse, who takes so many journeys through life with me in ministry and not once does he complain. He is truly my natural and loving king.

PREFACE

What if you had the opportunity to do life all over again? What would you do differently, if anything? Many of us live with regrets from the past and the choices we've made. Before you beat up on yourself, let me provide you with a few things to think about. No matter what choices we have made, good or bad, there is a lesson to learn from them. I wish I could say I made all the right choices in life so that my walk through life could have been seamless and without heartache; however, that was not the case and I am sure that is not life's story for many of you. Life has a way of taking us through valleys as well as mountaintops. While we enjoy the mountaintop experiences, it's really the valley experiences that bring out the best in us. These valley experiences create who we are and will bring us to our expected end.

God has designed us with a purpose in mind. To arrive at our purpose, we must go through a series of ups and downs to be effective and make an impact. The Bible clearly outlines many who have gone through valleys and trenches, close to death, to make it to the place He prepared for them to operate in purpose. Joseph was sold into slavery to the Ishmaelites by his jealous brothers just so, years later, he could save the lives of his father and brothers by preventing them from starving. Job was a good and upright man, minding his own business and just doing life as he knew how, when out of nowhere, his life was turned upside down by the loss of everything, including family and wealth. Naomi suffered the loss of all her family and was left alone in a foreign land with only her sorrows. How was she to know she would lose her spouse and children in a land that did not even worship her God? Hannah consistently prayed for God to bless her with a child because she was barren and constantly ridiculed by her husband's other wives, who all had children. God used her barrenness to bring life to many others through her prayers as she was blessed with a son named Samuel, who would spend all the days of his life in the temple of God. The Bible has reference after reference about the people of God going through valleys only so He can illuminate their purpose someday for going through the pain.

God may be allowing you to go through valleys now as well but hold on. Your mountaintop experience is on the way. Please do not let the trials of your lives be wasted by missing the turning point God is taking you to so you can be someone else's answer to life. Many people are waiting for the gifts God has planted inside of you to operate in purpose. Some of us have dealt with infant and pregnancy loss, infertility, or the death of a loved one who was closer to us than anyone could imagine. We feel grief from the hole that has been left in our hearts. We suffer from health issues where we had to fight for our lives, we endure divorce and infidelity, and we might have wayward children who have lost their way in life. The list can be endless.

Nevertheless, God has it all under control. He has given us

the tools to endure our valleys and enjoy our mountaintops. When we understand that the valley is temporal, we can enjoy our "now" because we know the future involves a mountaintop experience. Every trial we make it through is a revelation of who God is and a roadmap to help someone else navigate through their valleys and find freedom.

For years, God gave me the passage of scripture found in Isaiah 61:1-3, which says, "He anointed me to bring good news to the humbled and afflicted and to bind up the brokenhearted and release those who are in prison. He anointed me to proclaim the favorable year of the Lord, to comfort those who mourn and give them beauty for ashes, the oil of joy for mourning, and a garment of praise." These scriptures let us know that the world has trouble to offer, both to ourselves and others. We cannot be any of the things in the aforementioned scriptures unless we have endured the heartaches ourselves.

Will you join me in taking your heartaches and the trials of life and using them for the lifting of someone else? In other words, will you use the gifts that you have gained through your trials in life for a dynamic purpose orchestrated by God? Will you become that woman with purpose and make a difference for others who may be looking for answers to life's problems?

INTRODUCTION TO THE JOURNEY

It is natural for us to hold on to the negative and remember all the wrong things that have been done to us, but those things only hinder the path to the great purpose God has designed for each of us. We will begin our journey by admitting to the things that have hurt us, and by accepting that pain and disappointment have happened with an understanding that those things cannot continue to keep us bound. We must realize that we are not our circumstances—we are fearfully and wonderfully made. We are who God created us to be and we have the power to take back our lives and use those circumstances to turn the pain into purpose. The enemy desires to take the pain and break us but God has a different plan to bring us to a place where we can bring Him glory. He has a specific journey in life for each of us to travel and He has already created us for purpose.

This book is a Bible-based journey that provides twelve chapters of practical information to guide you to your freedom and restoration. As you read, you will be required to reflect on and work through things you may have considered nonexistent or which you have chosen to bury or ignore. One of the greatest things in life is the need to be free—free from pain, free from hurt, free from bondage, and free from the baggage that has hindered our walk through life and the ability to be lifted from the valleys. It is my hope that you will be free continually, will fight for your freedom, and that you will discover your purpose from the pain and free others in return. I will never be able to reach all the hurting women, just as Jesus in His natural form wasn't able to reach all those who were lost by physically visiting them, but after you become free, I hope that you will seek to help others shed the yokes of bondage. Although this book focuses more on women, there are countless men as well who are waiting for you to share your story and lead them to freedom.

Though our stories may be different, my story is one of feeling unloved, experiencing loneliness through lost relationships, and the pain of feeling emotionally abused at the hands of several people. I will share my journey to freedom with you as you read through this book, as I often speak about how I was let down by those I thought would love me just as God loves me. In my journey, many lessons were learned about love and how different the approach to love can be as we each find and define love. Some people might term being let down over and over by people as looking for love in all the wrong places. I had to fight for my freedom. My hope is after you have traveled through the chapters of this book, you will let go and let God be your source, and that He will have full control of your life and your purpose for being born into the Earth. Let your end be greater than the beginning as you walk in peace and purpose through this taxing journey called life.

Taking this journey to discover purpose requires you to seek comfort in scriptures, comfort in others, and making difficult, even painful decisions as you press forward. At the end of this book, it is my prayer that you are not only completely healed from your wounds of the past, but that you will know the true purpose of the pain. Remember Joseph in the book of Genesis who went from pain to prison to the palace. He was only seventeen when he was sold into slavery by his jealous brothers (Genesis 37:18-36). He never expected to one day be treated with such hatred by those who were supposed to love him the most since they were all a part of the same household.

If you are in the midst of your pain or even in an emotional prison, my prayer is that you will land in your palace through this freedom journey. Let's embark upon this journey together as we are our sister's keeper.

1

Feeling Loved

HAVE you ever asked yourself, "How can life be this painful and difficult?" You feel like you say all the right things and go to all the right places, yet something is lacking. You cannot quite understand the feelings you have that just drain you and sometimes leave you feeling hopeless.

You are certainly not alone. There are countless women just like you who feel that they have lost their way in life or simply didn't understand the path in the first place. Nothing has worked in the past or is currently working the way they planned. I certainly didn't ask for or plan the life I have had to journey through. Life was great when things were going well but there are always moments of heartache that come along and cause you to lose heart and want to give up. There were times when I had to choose between feeding myself or feeding my toddler. Yet, God said count it all joy (I am paraphrasing here) when you find yourself in countless measures that cut to your very core.

The beauty is that there are better things ahead as the valleys eventually turn into mountaintop experiences and you become intentional about discovering "your better" or whatever is best for you. **One of the first steps in discovering what is best for you is to understand that you are loved and valued by God.**

I somehow lost the revelation that I was loved by God and while going through such a dark and lonely place in my life, it took a while to feel loved and valued again. After my journey to freedom, I now know that God loves us with an everlasting love that no man or woman can measure or defeat. He loves us regardless of the circumstances in which we find ourselves. He loves us when others who say they love us or promise to love us in return do otherwise. He loves us whether we are on the mountaintop or in the valleys of life. He loves us regardless of whether we receive His love or not. He just loves us.

Not only is this a reality but it is up to each of us to receive this God-given love and walk in it. It is also wise to understand that He wants us to love ourselves. When we love and value ourselves, we place a whole new emphasis on life and its meaning. We begin to live and not merely travel through life, simply existing. Loving ourselves should never be unbalanced. We should understand that loving ourselves brings us a sense of peace and joy. In loving oneself, we accept who we are as individuals.

Why is it that we, as women, always seem to compare ourselves to other women? Can't we just accept who God created us to be and that it was His choice to make us tall or short, dark or light, have straight hair or curly/kinky hair, big hips or no hips, bubbly personality or restrained, the gift of gab or quiet? When we think of all these things and consider how He created us, we will learn to accept the person we have been made to be and walk joyfully in these things. What has happened is we have allowed the world to determine who we are and who we should be. We are who we are, and we are made the way we are made because God designed us to be a perfect picture of His Glory. His Glory is supposed to shine through us.

Please stop comparing yourself to others and give God thanks for His infinite wisdom in how He designed you. We have been fashioned and fit according to His image and His love for us. The only person others should see when they look at us is God and His Glory. Think about this and ponder these words for a moment. Jeremiah 1: 5 says that before you were even born and formed in your mother's womb, God knew you and He set you apart. Don't you realize that He was the one that formed you? Don't you realize that He knew exactly how He wanted to make you? Oh, how wonderful it is to honor God, who has taken the time to create every cell in our bodies, the hair on our heads, and the color of our eyes and skin, just the way He wanted us to be. When we allow this to truly soak in, we understand that no one person is better than another. We are all created in His image and after His likeness.

The truth is, we allow the enemy to tell us that others are better because of the way God has fashioned them, and that the materialistic things that others have amassed in this world somehow make them more favorable. While this may be true in the eyes of man, it is not so with God. May I suggest that we not follow the dreams that others have and follow the dreams and purpose that God has uniquely and individually given to each of us? This way we can stop following our feelings because feelings lead us astray almost every time. This path does not lead us to loving ourselves, but to comparing ourselves to someone else or succumbing to the feeling that we are inadequate or unloved based on another person's journey in life.

Love from God is not based on a feeling or even feelings that others must validate us. When we take our life and place the ability to be loved in another person's hands, we risk being grossly disappointed. You see, there are times when you feel you are at your worst moment in life and automatically think, *If I could just have their house (or their wardrobe, their appearance, or find a special person who will love me and I can spend the rest of my life with) then I would be the happiest person in the world.* The only problem with that is another human is not capable of producing this type of love for us. Unfortunately, humans are flawed and will act as such. Only God has the capability of truly loving us and drawing us unto Himself because inside all of us is a place that only God can fill. True feelings of love and joy come solely from God and things in the Earth can only bring us temporary moments of happiness, never the love and joy we immensely desire.

I learned this the hard way during my journey, until one day the Holy Spirit spoke to me and said, "You are depending on man to do a job that only I can do."

The person you are relying on to be your everything needs the same fulfillment you do. When two people are broken and neither knows how to provide the love the other so desperately desires, there is potential for loneliness and feelings of unfulfillment. Let me share a story with you about feeling loved or valued and how it can end up being less than what you think it might be. Yet, it has purpose.

Falling in love with another human being seems so easy. In fact, it feels natural and just flows in the beginning stages. There may be times when it feels like the two of you are inseparable as a man and woman who want so many things in life. You share the same big dreams that most everyone else does. You love each other as best you know how from a human perspective. But as Christians in love, so much time is spent going to church and not nearly enough time learning about the God we are supposedly worshipping and serving.

What happens when, over time, the love seems to fade as those in love grow emotionally farther apart? Though growing farther apart emotionally seems difficult, these moments become an opportunity to draw closer to the Father spiritually. It is easy to become exhausted as we try to "fix" each other, believing that the other person is always the problem. It is often hard to feel loved by each other and it is even more difficult to understand how to recognize the love of God for you as individuals. This is where I want you to understand that although we are to love each other as humans, real love can only come from God. We must stop searching for love outside of Jesus and seek to find it in Him first.

God gave us Jesus Christ to die for us so that we might have a relationship with the Father first, then ultimately with mankind. When we choose to accept the love God has provided for us through all eternity, we can move forward in life and love ourselves, instead of depending on others to provide what only God can give. Now, I know you hurt when you feel unloved and that is understandable from a human perspective. So, please don't feel like you should not expect to be loved by another person. It's just that man doesn't have the capability to love us like God loves us.

God has provided us with natural man to have meaningful relationships with and to replenish the Earth. He wants us to love others, but He does not want us to love others more than we love Him. The Word of God tells us in Mark 12:30-31 to love God with all your heart and with all your soul, with all your mind and with all your strength. The second is to love your neighbor as yourself. There are no greater commandments than these.

You see, God wants us to give and receive love. That includes loving another human as we desire and create relationships with each other as friends and as husband and wife. After some of us going through the journey of what we call "falling in love" found that things didn't work out quite like we planned, we had no choice but to run into the arms of Jesus. Jesus should be—or at this point, He should *become*—our everything. This is how we can live out Mark 12:30-31.

Our journey to purpose can stem from feelings of being unloved. When we no longer feel loved by man, we are left alone with our Heavenly Father and may be forced to talk with Him, as He is often the only one who is left in the silence and despair. Living with despair can be lonely and heartbreaking. I have felt unloved and have experienced moments of hopelessness from these feelings. My heart was truly broken from feeling unloved and discarded, and I felt like death was taking too long to come. Now, this does not mean I considered suicide because I never contemplated it—it just meant that I felt like I was dying a slow death inside while I watched my dreams fall apart before my eyes. I wanted to feel like I was wanted and not discarded. I wanted to have a genuine smile and not a smile that I had to hide behind, pretending to be okay. I wanted my heart to be unbroken.

I was raising three wonderful girls and life was hard. I had times when I was not only empty and lonely but was financially struggling and wanting so many things for myself and my girls. It always seemed like there was one problem or bad thing after another happening in my life. I hated wondering whether I would be able to keep the lights on in the house, buy clothes for the girls, or just keep food on the table. I wanted vacations and to be able to visit my family, who lived many miles away. It also never failed that every time I seemed to get slightly ahead, the car would need repairs. Yet, though I was facing all of this, I think the most difficult things were the feelings of overwhelming loneliness and rejection I went to bed with every night, leaving me to feel constantly unloved.

During all of this, I learned that love is not just a feeling. It is a choice to love another person even when the person doesn't respond the way we think they should. Love should be constant, intense, and so powerful that no one can break its bond. I learned to love God in this manner while I was left alone in these moments of misery and grief caused by people I loved more than God (if I am honest) just walking out of my life without looking back. I had to trust that God would never leave me, and I had to trust His Word when He said He would never forsake me. I was becoming weaker and weaker, both physically and emotionally, from all the disappointments that surrounded me. We are all weak when we find ourselves in these moments of life but if we trust God, we are made strong in our weaknesses. It should be more important how God views us during these times of disappointment.

So, how does God see you in your moments of disappointment? He looks at you with the same love and intensity as He did before you were born and before you were formed in your mother's womb. God had already claimed you as His very own and saw the great woman of purpose you would be someday. He knew you would go through seasons of feeling unloved, rejected, and devalued as a person. None of what you are experiencing is a surprise to God. He is using the pain and disappointment of every moment you did not feel loved to propel you to a place in Him that you could not imagine.

God uses our failures to promote us. He uses our pain to bring healing to others. The key to moving through these areas of pain and disappointment is to develop a relationship with the One who loved you first. He knows all about what you are experiencing and what is just around the corner for you. He has mapped out the course of your life and created a purpose in you far greater than your natural mind can comprehend. Getting you to that purpose in life will require your participation to say yes to Him and no to yourself, so He can bring you to your destination in life. When you have landed in your purpose, you will know the depth and breadth of His love for you.

There is no other love like the love the Father has for His children. Ephesians 3:17-19 tells us to be rooted and established in love that we may have power together with the Lord's holy people. To grasp how wide and long and high and deep is the love of Christ that surpasses knowledge, so you may be filled with all the fullness of God.

So, your pain and disappointment are not to remain rooted in bitterness, but rather to come to know the God of Heaven and fulfill your God-designed purpose. Step out on His love for you and choose to accept His plan for your life. Prove God at His Word. He will honor His Word as He protects His Holy and righteous name. You will then feel loved and valued beyond anything you can imagine.

Consider this and how valuable you are to God. Do you think He just created us because He was bored one day and said, "Let us make man"? Certainly not. He wanted us to be a member of His family. He wants to love and accept us as members of the family. Sometimes it is easy to feel loved but there are times when we find ourselves in low points in life where we question God's love for us. We should settle in our hearts that He loves us.

The truth that helps us settle His love for us is the death of Jesus on the Cross. There is no denying, and nothing can erase the fact that Jesus died on the Cross for us and that His love is eternal. John 15:13 says "There is no greater love than this, that a man should lay down His life for His friends." Jesus gave up His life for us so that we could have the opportunity to live. Since we have been given this kind of unselfish love, let us love ourselves and let us love others.

We must soley stop searching for love outside of Jesus and seek to find it in Him first!

2

Accepting Christ

BEFORE you can truly feel loved, you must know that you belong. What does it mean to belong when you feel like an outsider? Well, technically, we are all outsiders in this world. God has created us to live in the Earth but we are not from here. We are citizens of Heaven having an earthly experience. When we understand this, we understand to whom we belong.

Have you ever asked yourself, what am I doing here? What is my reason for being here? "Here" can mean on Earth or in whatever place you are currently sitting or standing. Why was I born in this generation? How did I end up in this city? In this home? Why was I sent to Earth?

These are all valid questions because even if you never

realized it, you are away from home and (hopefully) will someday return. The only way to return is to truly accept Christ as your Lord and Savior and His death on the Cross. We must accept what the Cross means and how Jesus paid for our sins to purchase us back to the Father with His own blood, pain, and agony. For some of you, this has probably already happened. For others, you might have an idea who Christ is through what you have been taught or heard from others over the years, but please settle for yourself, at this very moment, who He truly is from the Word of God.

It may be worth asking yourself, *What is my vision of Christ and how do I view Him?* We often see images of Him that others have created through some form of art. In other words, many have given Christ a physical form and have conveyed what their mental picture may be. That is not what I am referring to here. What is YOUR vision of Christ? Do you view Christ as the Son of God and that His purpose was to redeem you from sin and death and point you back to the Father? Consider His purpose, how short His life was, how much affliction He suffered during His time here on Earth, and the feat of the Cross. He went through pain in fulfilling His purpose for us so that someday we would be able to return home.

Philippians 3:20 says we are citizens of Heaven where Christ lives, and we are eagerly waiting for His return as our Savior. You must consider how Christ feels about you. I believe it is evident that His love for the Father and us is immeasurable. When it is impossible to receive this love because the circumstances in our lives have caused us to have a distorted view of God, we must examine all the circumstances and determine whether they outweigh His love for us. Is it possible that past hurt and pain have caused us to question God's existence or even His love for us?

I have often heard the question, "How can a loving God allow so many bad things to happen?" You have probably stated this at one time or another, or may be saying to yourself at this very moment, "Where are you, God? And when will things get better for me? How much more can I bear?" or "Do you even notice or care that I am hurting, God?"

Don't give up now. You are just beginning the journey toward wholeness. **If all the negative circumstances in your life lead you to a place in God where you can see His hand, you are headed in the right direction.** These circumstances build character, strength, and faith in you so you can be effective in your purpose.

The first step to being effective in your purpose is accepting Christ and the price He paid on the Cross for you. Without the Cross, there is no fulfillment of His promises to bring you joy, peace, and patience in the circumstances you face. We must remember that we are God's greatest prized possessions. He is only working out the kinks so He can use us for His Glory. Have faith that He knows what He is doing, even in the midst of your pain and circumstances.

James 1:3 states "that the trying of your faith worketh patience." It's the trying part with which we have the most difficulty. It was very difficult for me to accept that my happiness was crumbling right in front of me when I no longer felt valued and needed. I was on top of the world and my life was heading in the right direction. I was educated. I had standards for living. I considered myself part of the elite. Then it all came crashing down around me. I never expected to end up alone, broke, and heartbroken. It was difficult to have something or someone I loved one day, and the next day have it far from me. I couldn't understand how it all happened so quickly. One day I was excited about life and the next day I was trying to figure out where my next meal was going to come from.

I remember realizing that I did not have any money and I had no job at the time. I was trying to determine how I was going to feed my daughter. So, I decided I needed to visit family around dinnertime just to make sure my daughter received a meal. I didn't eat because I didn't want to seem like a burden. I was awaiting the opportunity to receive government assistance for food and money. It would be another three days before that would happen. As you can guess, I survived being hungry. Yet, through it all, I learned who Christ really is (not just what I had been told) so I could walk with Him daily in confidence. I learned to study His Word like never before and I learned to walk by faith and not by the circumstances. I learned to march around my Jericho walls and keep quiet until it was time for me to shout. I learned that faith in God came by hearing and in order to hear, I sometimes needed to remain silent.

These were not things that were found in my teachings about Christ when I was growing up and attending church. These were things God taught me Himself, personally, as I sat in a room with the door shut and just listened. I felt like Job at times, sitting in a pot of ashes just nursing my wounds. I felt like those who I considered friends were feeling sorry for me, just like Job's friends in Job chapter 4 of the Bible.

The beauty in Job's story and mine is that all the things I had amassed, which didn't amount to much, were nothing compared to what I was about to gain in the coming months and years. I gained so much more through my pain by simply sitting in His presence and being forced to crucify my flesh daily just to get through the day and live. I had to stare into the face of the adversary and be judged as not being the person I was expected to be. I had to deal with the adversary in my mind telling me that I was not going to walk out of the pain and that I deserved where I currently was in life. I felt like I was being stripped daily of everything I valued as I watched it all crumble before my natural eyes. Just like Job, I needed the Sovereign God. I needed to trust like never before as I hung on by a thread with hope fading rapidly. I knew I wasn't perfect but I knew God was with me, so I turned my face toward Him and began looking for His assistance in my pain.

I created a secret place just for me and God so that I could receive Him for who He was. He never disappointed me. I needed the secret place to be special, so I cleaned out a very small room in my house where I could commune with God daily. This was nearly thirty years ago and I still have a special space for God and me today. It is not the same space as it was then but God became even more real to me in that little room as I sat there night after night, talking and listening to Him so intently. God did say some things that were hard for me to swallow while I was in that room, but I just listened and over time, accepted my own actions. The beauty is that God still says things that are hard to swallow, and there are times I want to put up a fight or even argue, but I know better because there is no way I will ever win against the Sovereign God.

Going through difficult times and reaching a point where you become desperate often leads to moments where faith and your dependence on God become a major area of focus in your life. So, walk through your painful moments understanding that He is God, and He is full of mercy and grace for the journey. If you have a relationship with Christ, you are well on your way to fulfilling your purpose. If you do not have a relationship with Christ, it is not too late to receive Him as Lord and Savior today, so you can know that your present circumstances, no matter how negative, are only temporary.

You can begin to see the vision God has for your life in fulfilling your purpose. It becomes easier to move past the pain and walk hand-in-hand with our Savior when you accept Him as Lord and Savior over every area of your life.

John 14:6 says Jesus said unto us: He is the way, the truth, and the life. No man comes to the Father except through Him. He wants so desperately to know you more personally. He wants to heal all your broken areas and make you whole again. He wants you to know you are special and that He created you on purpose, with a purpose in mind.

3

~~~

Walking Through My Painful Moments

WALKING through life with Jesus allows us the ability to bear pain in a better light. Since pain can sometimes stem from different avenues in life, we must rely on Jesus to assist us in bearing our pain. These avenues may be residue from the past or something you are experiencing at this very moment. It may be a divorce, domestic violence, a loved one who has an addiction, the loss of a child, loss of finances, sexual abuse, racial oppression, childhood hurts, not feeling like you are loved...the list goes on.

Pain cannot be denied and is subjective based on what a

person is feeling, both naturally and emotionally. The painful moments in our lives often leave us bruised and scarred if we do not know how to effectively walk through them. I walked through some of my pain for nearly twenty years until I understood that it was taking me down a road and through jungles I never wanted to traverse. Pain makes us so uncomfortable that we lash out at others and create boundaries and walls to make everything appear to be okay to the outsider when the reality is, we are often not okay.

It is perfectly all right to admit that we are not okay and to accept help for our healing. It is not okay to remain in a state of constant despair and to always be pretending while we are emotionally dying inside. When our painful moments constantly lead us to feelings of anger that affect our day-to-day living, we need to force ourselves to admit that we need assistance in walking through these times. I like to call it getting naked before God.

I had to spiritually assess myself to determine what areas in my life needed change. I still do a spiritual assessment daily on my walk with God. I do not always like what I find in my self-assessments, but they provide room for repentance and growth. I have determined that we can pretend to be anything we want to be, but only for so long. He already knows the things that affect us anyway, so why pretend we are spiritually and emotionally okay? Pretending only leads to hiding our pain, which interferes with the healing we could be receiving.

I have had countless conversations with women since I began this journey of wholeness and many of us have the same kind of pain. The source of our pain usually involves some type of relationship with another person. As women, it is often difficult to feel a sense of defeat and watch the wounds as they become apparent reflections of our loss and pain. We even fill the pews in churches every week and lift our hands, sing all the songs, pray all the prayers, and say all the appropriate amens. We look and smell good, and on the outside, we appear to have it together. We even fight all the way to church with our loved ones, spouses, or children; then, as soon as we park the car on what we consider to be holy ground, we put on the fake smile, and say the halleluiahs and praise the Lords so that others can view us as someone we are not.

What we really need to do is fall on the altar and cry out for deliverance from the pain of the past or the current moment so we can receive our healing. Before any deliverance can take place, we first must admit we have the pain and that we need deliverance. Who are we fooling, anyway? We are attempting to hide the truth from others.

People often referred to me as having my life together and things were going well for me in my relationships with man and God. If only they knew I cried often until I had no tears left and I just became numb. Wounds tend to do that, you know. When you sever all the nerves in an area, the soreness lasts for only the moment of the severing. After the severing, you reach a place where there is only numbness and loss of feeling. Finding ourselves in a place of numbness leads us to hide behind our jobs, religious activities, and self-confidence to create an atmosphere that all is well. Well, we must learn to say all is *not* well and to shout from the rooftops that we need healing from the pain we have been carrying for way too long. We need healing for our souls so we can move on in life and be effective in our walk with God.

Let me share some of my journey on feeling unloved and why healing was, and is, imperative. I was at work one Sunday and began to feel dizzy and weak. I then began to have a bitter taste in my mouth followed by a cough. The next thing I knew,

I was waking up and found myself on the floor. I had fainted. I was unsure how long I had been unconscious. I just remember not feeling well before I fainted. It was close to the end of my workday, so I finished my day and went home without saying a word to anyone.

On Monday, I explained my symptoms to one of the physicians I worked with, and how my previous workday had unfolded. He decided to conduct a series of medical examinations on my heart. The results of the examinations determined that I had developed mitral valve prolapse caused by the undue amounts of stress I was experiencing at the time. So, not only was I dying emotionally, I was at risk for dying physically. The task of trying to hold it all together and remain emotionally stable was taking its toll on me. It was becoming evident that I would have to make changes to my current life if I wanted to live.

Pain is not meant to be held on to, but to be released so we can heal properly. Most of us present the façade of a beautifully painted portrait for the world to see, but when we flip the coin and really look at the back of our lives, things are a mess. We wear masks to shield others from the pain and heartache we experience. Our lives do not need to remain this way, but we must seek help and receive healing. We attempt to run from the pain or sever the pain through all kinds of avenues, like drugs, alcohol, and sadly, becoming engaged in even more toxic relationships, but the reality is unless we deal with the pain and walk through it effectively, we are just taking the pain everywhere we go because, unfortunately, WE are everywhere we go. No matter where you go, you and your brokenness will always be there. Ask God to heal you and to help you let go. Your life depends on it.

Most of us hold on to the pain because we are unforgiving

of those who hurt us. I want to encourage you to find a way to forgive and let go of the past. Yes, so many things have caused us to have valley experiences that have led us to face loss, and many of us have had relationships in life that fell apart. Some relationships were never really solid in the first place. However, when we make God our primary focus and let go of the unforgiveness and bitterness, He will take those ill feelings and pain and truly bless us with more than we could ever imagine.

In our experiences and disappointments in life, we tend to want to ponder our right to have solid, loving relationships with man, and to demand that someone else treat us a certain way because we think we deserve it. Truthfully, what do we deserve? What does another person owe us? Our whole being should be rooted and grounded in Christ. Yes, people make all kinds of promises to love, honor, and cherish us and sometimes those promises are not kept. In our own human fallacies, we make promises to others that we do not keep, causing others to walk through pain and disappointment. Whatever the reasons are, unfortunately, people are just people and we are all capable of making mistakes. We are capable of not keeping our word and letting others down. Therefore, the ability to have grace abounds. **Grace abounds through the work of Jesus and He is the answer in every situation.**

Jesus is the only answer to all our needs. Sometimes our needs are greater at certain times than others. Yet, He was sent to deliver us from the hand of the enemy and that includes the pain of this life.

The Word of God states in Psalms 34:19, "Many are the afflictions of the righteousness, but the Lord deliver us out of them all." So, expect to come out of your pain and not look like you've been in the fight of your life while enduring it. We have to understand that Jesus died for more than our ticket out of Hell. He died for so much more than that. He died so that we could have healing in all areas of our lives. Receive your healing from the pain and know that nothing is a surprise to God. He already knows about everything we are experiencing in life. Allow Him to heal your heart and restore your peace and joy, all while making you feel whole again.

A portion of your healing is done by considering what caused your pain and acknowledging that you are still hurting from that pain. Ask God to heal your hurt and set your mind and heart to forgive the one who caused the hurt.

Lamentations 3:22-23 says, the steadfast love of the Lord never stops, nor His mercies end. They are new every morning and great is His faithfulness.

God is waiting on us to decide that we have had enough of the status quo and holding on to the pain, disappointment, and unforgiveness so He can propel us to new and higher places in the Earth and in ministry for a major purpose.

Turn your attention away from the pain and disappointment in your life and place a greater focus on God and the promise of restoration and deliverance. Once you take this step, you enter into a divine relationship with God and He begins to rewrite the plot and story of your life. What the enemy meant for harm, God is using for a purpose that will blow your mind. God will begin to walk through the valleys with you as well as the mountaintops. He will breathe new life into your dead situations and begin to sow seeds of greatness and destiny into your life. The key is to begin to cultivate these seeds and allow them to take root to replace the pain and disappointment so you can reap a harvest of healing, peace, and joy. God will begin to restore His original plan for your life.

We must remember that Christ also experienced pain, agony,

and disappointment as He walked this Earth and ultimately endured the Cross. Therefore, everything we experience, He has also already conquered. Every tear we've cried, He was aware. Every pain we felt, He was aware. Our pain is now His pain. Our war wounds from being in the fight of life are now His war wounds. Our victory is now His victory. He conquered all things long before we were born. He gave us victory over every situation over 2,000 years ago. So, why are we still holding on to the things He has already overcome? There is nothing that we can go through that God cannot heal.

So, if you have cried (and I am sure you have, and maybe are doing so at this moment), know that it's okay to cry. It's even okay to bellow out a scream if you must. But remember, at the end of the day, God is always with us and He is concerned about the pain and disappointment we experience. He may even be allowing our pain and disappointments as trials to reveal His character in us even though He has already taken care of those trials.

I can truly say that I am thankful for my trials now, although I wasn't thankful when I was in the midst of them. I learned to be so content at one point that it was frightening to be so calm. Not one thing about my situation had changed. In fact, it began to get worse when I went into my secret closet to get naked before God and pour out my heart. But God began to give me an utterly inexplicable peace. I had medicated myself on a form of church and toxic, earthly relationships trying to find some structure of joy and happiness. God allowed me to go through all of it and to literally wear myself out before coming into the true and loving relationship with Him because I was devoid of options, having already tried to fix problems that were well beyond my qualifications. I was wearing my physical self into exhaustion and my body was breaking down faster than I could imagine. I was constantly ill, whereas I had been a very healthy person until this time. I was admitted to the hospital twice with heart-related issues, which have all resolved since I became free.

I had to choose to live and not die, I had to choose to let go and let God. I had to choose freedom from the pain and unforgiveness. I had to choose to step out of the boat and walk on the water to come to Jesus even when the sea was raging. I had to choose to see His hand reaching out for me. The only thing that kept me from drowning was to continuously keep my eyes on Jesus.

We all go through pain and disappointment because we live in a fallen world. We are not immune to the valleys of suffering and pain, no matter how much we would like to be on the mountaintop. How we respond to our suffering and pain reveals a lot about our trust in Him. When we respond to the voice of the enemy and how he wants us to resolve a situation, we only make our situations worse. We must remember that God has power over all our circumstances, and if we release those circumstances, He is able to deliver us and set us free.

So, release your pain. Release your concerns. Release your unforgiveness. Release your grief from toxic relationships and other things that have brought you to the point of desperation. Release the spirit of rejection that attempts to attach itself to you when you experience painful moments. Jesus wants to bear all these losses for you. He was wounded and bruised for your healing and that includes your emotional, mental, physical, and spiritual healing. He is here for you and wants to give you a rest as you walk through and relinquish your pain to Him. He even wants to help you in your moments of grief or whatever areas of your life feel like heavy burdens, such as the stress, anxiety, and oppression you are constantly carrying.

We suffer so many losses throughout our lifetime and each

time we are required to adapt to the grief. We find it difficult to understand, yet we adapt to things like the death of a loved one when we trust God and allow time to pass. However, most people never consider the loss of a meaningful relationship with another person as something that is grieved. Loss is loss and yes, we grieve relationships that have fallen apart no matter the reason. A part of you will feel broken and lost like no one could ever imagine unless they have experienced the same pain. The burden can become so heavy and overwhelming that you may not know how you will make it another day living apart from the love of God.

Before I developed this relationship, I lived every day in a fog. I pretended a lot because I didn't want to face the reality I was living. I liked pretending better because I felt safe as long as no one knew I was failing at life. So, I continued to go to work each day and gave one hundred percent of myself to my job. This helped to keep me from thinking about the burdens I carried around with me and the anguish I went to bed with each night. We were never equipped to carry such heavy burdens. We must draw closer to Him so we can let go of the pain and walk in purpose.

Walk in the purpose of restoring others who are in the midst of pain and unforgiveness. Don't be bothered if others do not receive your gift of healing through sharing your life story and how God healed you from the painful moments you've suffered. We must understand that some of us who are hurting are not ready to let go of the past and prefer to remember the wrongs that have been done to them. It takes longer for some to heal but God will heal them in His and their own time. Each of us walks through life at different paces. My prayer is that we learn how to forgive and to understand that forgiveness is a necessary path to total and complete healing. We can never fully heal until we forgive.

We will discuss forgiveness in more detail in a later chapter. For now, let's focus on healing and releasing the fact that we have been rejected.

4

~⚬~

Recognizing the Spirit of Rejection and Receiving Your Healing

THERE is a familiar parable in the Bible that we call "the Prodigal Son." The parable is found in Luke 15:11-32. There are many meanings to this parable, depending on how we read it and how the Holy Spirit interprets this passage to us. However, many of us read these scriptures as being about a son who was a sinner who came home to be saved and lived for the Kingdom of God after living a less-than-favorable life.

We also see the older brother as selfish and demeaning to

the brother we feel he should have embraced when he returned home. No doubt the older brother felt rejected because he had remained with the father and had done everything asked of him. He considered himself a responsible son. He didn't squander all his living trying to be someone he was not. He was just the perfect son in his own eyes.

We too feel mistreated when we do everything in our power to be decent and morally good, and do all the right things so others will be pleased with us. I want to share with you that we are *never* good enough that others will be pleased with us. People will always find some type of fault. I would like to say that I was perfect, that I do not know why I did not receive the love I desired, and that I should have been spared my unwarranted pain. Well, in that quiet room, God had to remind me that I was *not* perfect, and that I had to acknowledge *my* part in the things that led me to feelings of being unloved and unwelcomed.

If we are honest with ourselves, we will admit that some of the things we feel are from either the words we have spoken or the choices we have made against the will of God. When I wanted to talk with God about how I was hurt and how I was feeling let down, God listened without interruption until I was done. God then began to talk to me only about me. Of course, I felt like I was perfect, and I had so many qualities that others did not have. I guess you can say I was self-righteous. This is so out of order when it comes to how we see ourselves and the real truth. I can admit that I had a lot of room to grow in that season of my life. I still have room to grow today—albeit in different areas—to be who God has designed and called me to be in life.

I had to submit to God that there were many things I could have done better then and things I can do better now. I did not submit at first because I wanted God to know how angry, confused, and hurt I was at the pain and loneliness I felt. I wanted God to know that I was being rejected and He was telling me about my faults. I wanted Him to take the focus off me and work on those who had disregarded the feelings of His daughter. Doesn't that sound so "holy" and self-righteous? We often say things like, "God got me because He don't like ugly." Yes, God does have us, but we must face the reality that even though we might be hurting, we must examine ourselves to determine whether we need changes or improvement.

Not all of us have played a part and some of us have truly been wronged. Yes, we have been rejected and God does not take that lightly. Rejection is a bitter pill to swallow. I am asking that we release ourselves from the spirit of rejection, as it has the potential to destroy us if we do not let it go.

If I had to give a definition from experience, *rejection* can be defined as discarding another as though they do not matter and declining to receive their love and affection. I am sure you can also take this definition and add your own story to it. There have been times that the spirit of rejection has invaded our lives and made us feel less than or weak and vulnerable. The spirit of rejection not only makes us feel like we are not worth anything, but there are so many more spirits that come along with the spirit of rejection. The rooted spirit of rejection has many branches and I am going to name just a few. Please let us examine ourselves to make sure that we are aware of these spirits and make every effort to gain freedom from the friends that accompany the spirit of rejection. It is my hope that we can release the scars of the past as we conquer the spirit of rejection.

The spirit of rejection brings with it loneliness, isolation, anger, insecurity, fear, anxiety, resentment, rebellion, lack of trust, and sometimes rage to the point that it destroys potential new relationships and causes loss of confidence. The spirit of rejection sabotages new relationships because we create barriers for others and live in the shadow of those who rejected us.

I had baggage when I moved on to new relationships. I purposed in my heart that no one would ever make me feel unwanted again. I have a dominant personality by nature and that made it harder to destroy the wall of insecurity. I just knew I had to take care of myself because no one else was going to do it for me. I became Ms. Independent, so to speak. I wanted to reject others before they rejected me. What an awful place for a person so deserving, wanting to love and cherish us, to be placed in because we never denounced the spirit of rejection!

We must realize that in this life, and while we are in the natural realm of the Earth, we are subject to rejection. We may be rejected for job promotions, relationships with friends and spouses, as well as children who decide they no longer need us as overbearing parents. **Working to be free of rejection is a daily walk.** We must make every effort to "let it go."

This is not an effort that can be accomplished on our own. We must be subject to the Holy Spirit and His Anointing. We are incapable of letting go that easily. There will be much prayer and trust in the Word of God to be free from such a stronghold because it is the root of the tree. Some roots go very deep, especially the longer we allow the spirit of rejection to devour our lives. My advice is to employ the Word of God to replace the tree—chop it down and go even further and dig up the roots. Until then, we will feel unwanted, unloved, and unaccepted, which makes us always seeking to go the extra mile—to the point of exhaustion—trying to please others in hopes they will like us or make us feel valued.

This is a mental stronghold you can be free of. You are God's masterpiece and you deserve to walk in total freedom from anxiety, fear, and rejection. It is vitally important that we address this spirit and tackle it daily to remain free in the bondage of our minds. We cannot walk in our full potential and God-given purpose until we are walking in total freedom. The good news is that God understands rejection and wants to set us free. Remember that when Jesus walked the Earth among his very own, and even when He hung on the Cross, He was rejected by many. Therefore, we are not leaning on Him for anything He has not already walked through.

Ask yourself if you have a spirit of rejection. I have listed many other spirits that are associated with the spirit of rejection. I encourage you to examine your past carefully for things like whether you have experienced a marriage betrayal or divorce, you have parents who divorced when you were a child and you had to live through it, you have a parent who walked away from you when you were a child, or you have been passed over for a promotion or feel that you have been discriminated against at a job. Now, examine how it makes you feel just thinking about these things. If you are angry or certain people come to mind, you may have been rejected and you might want to consider forgiving those who rejected you. This means that a true conversation is needed to regain your freedom, so you might have to call or meet the person face-to-face to regain that freedom.

Releasing the spirit of rejection brings us the freedom to walk in destiny and purpose. Though Christ was rejected, He became the head cornerstone (Psalm 118:22). How much is He concerned about you and your experience of being rejected? Release the spirit of rejection and watch yourself soar to the top. The spirit of rejection causes us to strive for what we get, and we find ourselves busy attempting to make others notice how important we are and how valuable we can be. The reality is, we are no more important than the Great One who lives inside of us.

The spirit of rejection robs us of our ability to rest because we always feel like we have something to prove to others so they can view us as worthy. But we are already worthy because God says we are, not because man must validate our worth. God says that we are His and He loves us—not because of anything we have done but because we are His children. He loves us to the point that He wants us to be free from the stronghold of the spirit of rejection.

Please stop holding on to the deep-rooted spirit of rejection and its branches, and allow the authority and truth found in the blood of Jesus to make you whole again. Walk in love. Walk in total freedom. Walk freely away from the spirit of rejection. Walk in forgiveness.

5

Untying the Yoke
of Unforgiveness

WALKING in forgiveness means finding out where we are hurt and broken. Brokenness leaves our hearts and lives shattered in a million pieces. It's so difficult to put them back together sometimes, and there is not enough superglue in the world to take us back to where we were before our lives were shattered. And every shattered piece often has another person's name attached to it.

The problem isn't that we are broken. The problem is how we allow ourselves to *remain* broken. Sometimes we remain broken because we do not understand how we became broken in the first place. Because we do not have an understanding, we are left in a state of confusion with no point of reference to begin to put the pieces back in place. Yet we must pick up the pieces and do something to regain some form of normalcy. Picking up the pieces after we've been broken is not an easy task. It is not a task we should tackle alone nor should we desire to do so. We must seek God's guidance and wisdom for the path before us. Only He has all the answers to place every broken piece back in its rightful place.

I wanted my heart to not be broken anymore. I wanted my life to be one of peace, happiness, and love. I wanted to feel like I mattered. I didn't want to be discarded like I didn't belong and as if I did not matter in life. I was human. I had feelings. I was created by God. Yet there I was with a heart that ached so badly that I cornered myself in my mind just to keep others from hurting me even more. I wanted to scream at everyone who didn't understand the pain and heartache I felt. I wanted to find the people who left me feeling unloved and say to them, "Don't you know what I am going through?" and "Don't you care how I feel?"

But I did not do any of these things. I just remained trapped and bound, trying to figure out how I ended up in a place of such misery and despair. No one deserves to feel like they are nobody. This life I was living was like constantly sucking on lemons. There was nothing sweet and loving about it.

We have all heard the phrase, "When life hands you lemons, make lemonade." Well, I made my lemonade. However, I suggest we go a bit further. After we have made our lemonade, we should sit in God's presence and savor the taste, like it is the best thing we have ever had. That way, no one can say we are sucking on sour lemons and continuing to live bound by the yoke of unforgiveness. That truly is what is happening when we dwell on the past. We are just holding our lemons in our hands and pondering the sour deeds that have been done to us. The sad thing is, we don't realize that many times, the person who has brought us pain has moved on with their lives. Now, this is not to discredit that we have been wronged. Far from it. I will be the first to say that I held on to my lemons until some of them rotted and dried up. When all was said and done, I almost didn't have enough lemons left to make my lemonade.

Thankfully, I realized that holding on to unforgiveness was only making me sick. I would be lying if I said that there were days I did not even want to get out of bed, much less squeeze a lemon and make lemonade. I wanted to take my lemons and rub them in the faces of those who had hurt me and see if they could feel the things I was feeling. I wanted their lives to be as sour as mine was at the moment.

None of that happened, of course, and God began to speak to me and teach me how to carefully slice and squeeze my lemons to make the most of my situation. It was then that I was able to place the shattered pieces in some form that made sense and allowed my life to have meaning again. I wish I could say this happened overnight or even in a few weeks, but it was years before I was normal again. It took a lot of praying and pushing myself to move beyond the broken pieces by putting each piece back into its proper place. I was never the same as I was before the brokenness, but I later learned that was a good thing. Just like any delicate thing that has been broken, it is never the same, even though great care was taken to put it back together.

God allowed the brokenness to take place so I could be the person He purposed me to be. God did not *cause* it to happen, He *allowed* me to be broken at the hands of others. I pray that you can make the most of your situation as well, no matter how hard it seems, so you can walk in your purpose and find peace along the journey as you allow the yokes to fall off of your life.

Think about a yoke and what it does. It acts as a harness that binds you to something. **Unforgiveness can be a yoke that binds us to our past and we just keep pulling our shattered pieces around with us.** We keep dragging situations and people along the journey when they were meant to be left behind long ago. They were there for a season, but they certainly do not fit into the plan and purpose God has for us now. They become the shattered pieces of our lives that we should never try to put back together. So many of our shattered pieces have other's names attached to them. We even walk on these shattered pieces or hold them in our hands. When we are angry, we clench our hands so tight that we bleed from the shattered pieces. We must open our hands and let go of the shattered pieces and the reins of life so Jesus can bring us our freedom, which He has already paid for on our behalf.

We are so special to God that He wants us to be free from bondage, free from past hurts, free from sour lemons, and free from unforgiveness. So, if we find ourselves keeping a running list of who has hurt us in the past, we are walking in unforgiveness. Our Heavenly Father says that we should forgive others as we have been forgiven. I did not write these words and we are not able to rewrite the Word of God under any circumstances, whether we like what He says or not. His Word is not open for debate.

I know it is difficult sometimes to just let go of past hurts and how badly we have been treated. For me, it is a lifelong process. I must be cognizant of this daily to remind myself that I must forgive. In our journey toward forgiveness, it may be helpful to seek God for a person with whom we can share our pain and release the people in our lives who need our forgiveness. After all, we are also human, and I am sure we have wronged others, intentionally or unintentionally. We too need forgiveness.

When considering forgiving others, there are a few things we must ponder. We must think about who unforgiveness affects more, us or the person we need to forgive. I submit to you that we are being affected more. We are living the harsh life that keeps us bound in chains from all the bitterness and hurt another person has caused. Yet, we can walk free when we let others know that we forgive them, even if it is not received by them. It is often difficult to ask for forgiveness or to forgive others. But without forgiveness, we remain yoked, chained, and bound. We become prisoners locked inside our own beings.

Colossians 3:13 tells us that if any man quarrels against another, forgive them as Christ has forgiven us. We are not able to forgive in our own power but the Holy Spirit empowers us to forgive. One of the first steps to ignite this power is to admit that we are weak and that in order to obey God in forgiving others, we must depend on Him and His strength. We are mandated by the Word of God to forgive.

During what felt like countless years of excruciating pain and suffering, I had to have self-talks about how carrying unforgiveness was affecting me. I honestly did not think I could forgive. I wanted to move on so badly, but I also wanted things to change and go back to the way I perceived they were when my life seemed glorious. Looking back now, I know that my perception of a great life was one built on pretenses through highly toxic relationships—so toxic that in my moments of wanting to hold on to what I had, and also needing to let go, it was like a canker sore eating to my very core. I had to let go. I had to be free. I had no choice if I wanted to have the life God designed for me and to be loved the way I deserved to be loved.

Do not sell yourself short and settle for mediocrity. You

deserve God's best for your life too and moving beyond the yoke of unforgiveness opens the door for love to flow in abundance.

Let me share something with you about walking the path of forgiveness and how God operates when we live a life of love and forgiveness. Just when we think it is impossible to forgive, God brings us face-to-face with situations that test our ability to walk in faith. The Sovereign God knows exactly where we are in life and what we need to be able to move past the areas in our lives where we feel lost. During my many years of pain, I tried so hard to make things better on my own. I soon realized that the only thing that would help me heal was to let go of the past and look ahead to the future. God had so many things available for me that I never would have received had I held on to the pain and disappointments of the past. God constantly communicated with me and always revealed things to me so that I was never in the dark or unclear about any situation. The Holy Spirit spoke to me and made me aware that I was about to face another obstacle or reach a point of devastation in life, and He would give me the power to overcome somehow. I cried on so many people's shoulders that I am sure they were tired of seeing me coming.

One day, as I was praying, the Holy Spirit shared that I should prepare for heartbreak ahead and even provided me with scripture to confirm what He spoke to me. This was the very first time I knew something was not right in my life and that I was about to take a turn for the worse. God warned me because He loved me that much and He did not want me to be blindsided by what I was about to experience.

Even though God warned me, it was still difficult to walk through the valley of pain as I was not equipped for the battle. However, if God warned me then, I knew He had already made a way of escape. He gave me the strength to make it through the pain and gave me more strength to walk in forgiveness.

I am sure you can imagine how difficult it is to forgive when others cause us hurt, but God said we must forgive so we can be free. So, I forgave, picked up the pieces of my life, and moved on. I did not wish any malice to those who had caused me so much pain. In fact, I began praying that they would find what they were searching for in life because I knew what they were searching for was not on the outside, but within. I was able to forgive because I had already found the answer to what I was searching for. His name is Jesus and He cleansed all my ways and gave me a new path to freedom by helping me let go of the yolk of unforgiveness.

When I said to those who hurt me, "I forgive you," I was also saying to God, "I obey you because I value your Word, Lord, over my feelings." I realized that the longer I chose not to forgive, the more acrimonious I became. I was taking the place of God by not forgiving and hating those who had hurt and betrayed me by leaving me to feel pain and rejection. I only felt more miserable on top of the seeds of despair that had been sown in my life.

Please ask God to help you forgive if you need to do so for your freedom. Jesus has already paid the price for our freedom, so why give the power back to another person to yoke us in the bridles of unforgiveness?

Unforgiveness causes us to feel miserable and die a slow death. Those who have hurt us have power over us even when we are trying to detach ourselves from them. So, why don't we jump at the opportunity to forgive when we have been wronged? We are only hurting ourselves by not extending forgiveness to others as well as asking others for forgiveness.

One reason we don't easily forgive is because it makes us

look like we are the ones who have done wrong, and the other person wronged us because we deserved it. We feel like we are superior to the other person, and if we do not forgive, they will pay for what they have done to us. That is truly between them and God. Being angry and unforgiving doesn't speed up the process of what we feel should be their punishment. We are no better than the person who wronged us and we should not be seeking self-righteousness.

Forgiveness is the only way to get us through the hurt and pain from flawed relationships with man. Forgiveness is the only way to keep us from being held hostage by the pain of the past. Forgiveness gives us a new attitude and a clean slate. Only God has graced us to forgive and to be forgiven by others. So, let go of unforgiveness and bitterness and ask God to soften your heart so you can be free. Ask God to show you areas of unforgiveness in your life so you can openly denounce them and relinquish the yokes weighing you down and causing you even more pain. Consider for a moment what your life would be like if you just chose to forgive. Ask yourself if you have received God's forgiveness for yourself.

We can only give away what we have received ourselves. If we haven't received God's forgiveness, maybe that is a hindrance to our ability to forgive others. Receive His forgiveness toward us and our imperfections so that we can then forgive others. Forgiveness is hard work and I do not want to make it seem like it will just happen overnight. From my own experience, it doesn't—it is a process that leads to maturity and helps us forgive easily. There is a path to walking in forgiveness that is sometimes curvy, slippery, and steep. In our quest to forgive, we might fall off the path occasionally. Forgiveness is a daily walk as Jesus taught us to forgive each other in Matthew 18:22 not seven times, but seventy times seven.

Now, this does not mean that we should remain on the path of people who hurt us. It does mean that we must seek shelter to protect ourselves from those who continuously cause us pain. In my opinion, and for my situations, that just meant me walking away and never looking back. And while I walked away, I thanked God for my freedom to live again and to be free from pain, hurt, and unforgiveness.

Being free allows you to see your purpose more clearly and to focus on where God is leading you to make a difference in the Earth. Walking through the pain, experiencing the bitterness, and elevating to forgiveness is the path to wholeness and restoration that will allow you to freely walk in your purpose through the Sovereignty of God.

*Every trial we make it through
is a revelation of who God is!*

6

Breathing Again

FREELY walking in our purpose requires letting go and embracing the ruach of God. How invigorating it is, oh Lord, to be able to breathe the fresh air of your loving power! Job said in chapter 33 verse 4 that the Spirit of God made Him, and the breath of the Almighty gave him life. There is a serenity that comes from surrendering our lives and will to God. Being able to breathe again means surrendering to His presence and saying yes to His will. We must understand that God loves us and the only way to truly breathe again is to know there is joy, peace, strength, and love when we develop a personal relationship with Him. He is our sustainer in life and there is so much fulfillment just being in His presence.

God's presence allows us to remain connected to hope and joy in Him as we experience the pain and heartache this life has to offer. Unfortunately, pain and heartache are offered over and over without asking for them. Yet we must always settle the fact in our mind that God is always with us whether we choose to acknowledge Him or not. Psalm 139:8 says if I rise up in Heaven, He is there; and if I make my bed in Hell, He is there too. So where will we go to hide from God? There is not one place. He is omnipresent and I am grateful for Him always surrounding me with His presence.

When I went to my secret place with God during all those years of pain, as I was reaching the end of my rope and losing all hope that my life would ever be fulfilled, I found Him. He wasn't lost. He was just waiting on me to acknowledge that He was right there all the time. Every time I was wronged, He was there, heard every word, and saw every action. He heard me cry in the middle of the night and remembered all my tears shed in moments of despair. He helped me with my children when I wasn't sure how I would feed, clothe, or shelter them. I cried by myself because I did not want my girls to be affected by the shattered, lifeless life I was living daily. There were times when I was not sure where the next meal would come from or how the lights would remain on. Yet He sustained me through it all because I remained in His presence. And in His presence, I could breathe again.

I needed to be reminded often to breathe. I needed His presence to feel valued and loved. God is so much bigger than we can imagine. We place Him in the small spaces of our minds when He is far greater than all the things we reduce Him to. During those moments, as I learned to breathe again, I would just sit and listen to His voice. He would speak softly sometimes, and at other times He would just breathe His precious breath of life on me to sustain me. Then He showed me how to breathe.

Today, I am still breathing and as you are sharing this journey with me, I want you to breathe as well. God has it all under control. He is just waiting on us to step into His presence and sit and feel His powerful, glorious breath on us.

God is so powerful and majestic. As we draw close to Him, He heals all our pain, hurt, and desolation. If we do not learn how to sit in His presence, we continue to hold on to the past. Letting go is refreshing and liberating.

Let me take you on a journey of what happened in this room where God and I met daily. As my earthly trials intensified and it seemed as if I was going to breathe my last breath, my relationship with God began to take on new life. I would walk into the space I had created for me and God. This space had a desk, chair, floor lamp, and a few boxes of things I had never bothered to unpack when moving into this home over ten years earlier. The moment I opened the door, I could feel the Father breathe on me and I heard His voice clearly. I could *feel* His presence, which was so strong that I knew He was waiting on me to enter that place where He and I could commune. I would pray for a while. I would read the Word of God for a while. Then I would sit and listen for Him to tell me what was on His mind.

Sometimes He wouldn't speak for several minutes but when He did, He never ceased to tell me how much He loved me. He always let me know He was with me and that He would never leave me. He told me one day that I should be still and see the salvation of the Lord. I knew He meant that at that very moment, He was fighting every battle and not one thing that had wronged me had gone unnoticed. He also asked me to be forgiving and to treat the wrongs and those who had wronged me like they deserved to be loved, and to show them grace just as He has continuously shown me grace. I did not argue this point because I knew He was right, as He always was and continues to be.

I did have to pray for strength to keep smiling and walking in love. It became easier to do the more time I spent with Him in that little space that was just ours to share. I reached a point in my relationship with God where I couldn't wait to step into that room and close the door—not because I wasn't hurting anymore but because of His healing presence, outpouring, and breathing on me. I lost the desire to fight what I considered lost battles. I just fell in love with God daily and with that came so much peace. Nothing changed about the way my life was going and nothing else mattered. I simply met God daily and we became so close that nothing but being with Him seemed important.

God was so much greater than the problems I was facing. The religion instead of relationship I had practiced all those years began to fade and the newness of who He truly was became my foundation upon which to build my life. I now know what Paul meant when he said in Philippians 4:11 to "be content in whatsoever state I am in." I had no choice but to be content. I couldn't make any of my problems disappear or get better at that moment. Sadly, but now gratefully, I learned the power of loving God on a whole new level.

I visited that tiny space for what seemed like years—and it was at least five years of pain, tears, and heartache before God finally said to me, "It's time." He was saying it's time to move to a better place in life because I had been stagnant for years. It was time to walk away from the feelings of being unloved, the loss of hope, and despair. He was saying it was time to walk away from my current surroundings. It was time to reclaim my freedom. Time to breathe again.

I wasn't sure I was ready to take this step but I knew I had to obey. I wasn't even sure what I was walking into. However, when God said it was time, I knew He had already worked things out for me so I could obediently take these steps—just as God told Abram in Genesis 12:1 to leave his family and his country to go to a land that He would show him. He wanted Abram to take the next steps to a new beginning so He could make his name great. I too had to take the steps, and just like Abram, be obedient even though I wasn't sure about much at that moment except that I was to go. I had to step outside of the tent of confinement and be obedient in order to make the move for which I had been commanded.

Because I knew it was time to go, I began to step outside of my comfort zone and walk in faith that He would take me from the valley experiences to the mountaintop. I knew it was time to go because He said so, but I also knew I would have to reestablish a space for God and me to meet. My relationship with Him was that strong and that important. I can't breathe without His presence. I can't move without His presence. I can't live without His presence. It was His strength that got me through the difficult times. It was His power that allowed me to function and win in life every day. It was His wisdom that kept my path straight and my feet walking in the right direction.

Psalms 37: 23-24 says, "The steps of a good man are ordered by the Lord and he delighteth in his way. Though he fall, he will not be utterly cast down, for the Lord upholdeth him with His hand."

I fell a lot. Honestly, I even had a few choice words to say that may have been inappropriate until I began to commune with God in the space that was just ours. I became more consciously aware of His presence in my life. I knew without a doubt that He was with me everywhere I went and many times we didn't have to say a thing—I just knew He was right there beside me. I could feel His breath on me and His presence from within. I didn't have to battle anymore in the natural. I was able to conquer so much more as I was taught to battle in the Spirit.

Now, if you are battling issues at this moment in your life that are causing you pain and disappointment, I pray for your wholeness and restoration and the ability to walk away in forgiveness if that is what is needed. God does restore lives and mend hearts. I have no answer for why He did not restore my life the way I desired. I certainly prayed consistently for healing and restoration. I prayed harder than anyone can probably imagine. I am not sure why I prayed so hard, yet I am sure there were many reasons. Nevertheless, I still prayed. He then breathed on me. I did not get the answers I *desired* but received the answers I *needed* so that I too could breathe again. As I started to breathe again, I began to understand how important it was to show others how to breathe. It became one of my purposes.

My prayer for you is that you can freely breathe again as you walk through the unwanted and uninvited pain and disappointment this life has to offer, all while learning to love those who may not love you back.

7

Learning the Art of Loving the Outsiders

WHAT is love, you may ask, and how do we learn to love those who reject our love? Well, it depends on the kind of love you are speaking about. Love takes on different actions. *Agape* love is Godly or unconditional love in which we love others because God says so. *Eros* love means we have relational or romantic love for a spouse. *Phileo* love is brotherly love or love for our friends. What do you associate with love when you consider those who are different from you? How do we continue to love those who have caused us pain? What happens when there is no longer any eros love available?

There are so many questions and few answers. It is difficult to think about continuing to love someone when you must shift from agape and eros love to agape love. This means we must choose to love despite how we feel. John 15:12 says we are to love one another as He has loved us. This is not easy, and in fact, often seems impossible. It especially seems impossible in our own strength. It is only through a relationship with God that we can love unconditionally.

As our relationship develops with God, our relationships with others will change. The closer we become to the Father, the more we see others in a different way. This takes a bit more maturity in Him to be able to move past the hurt and pain of the past to be able to walk in love. Those who have hurt us have lost a space in our hearts and we now see them as outsiders. We must now learn the art of loving them as an outsider. They are now strangers to us and are no longer welcome in the innermost parts of our lives. We begin to feel as if the pain they caused us destroyed their right to be anything other than an outsider.

It is easy to become strangers with those who hurt us, and it often becomes impossible for us to show any kind of love toward them. It became easy for me to feel as if others didn't deserve my love because it had been proven over and over that I was not important and I was not a person worthy of their love. I wanted to know what the purpose was for them entering my life and making promises to love and cherish me if those promises were not going to be honored. I wanted to know why I was battling such feelings of loneliness at such a critical point, and how I had reached what seemed to be the lowest point in my life. I never got the answers to these questions and honestly, it really doesn't matter anymore. The reality is, I was not only at a low point, I also had to show love to every person who brought me pain and suffering.

Wow, that's something to think about and it was difficult to comprehend. I knew that likely no one cared about my feelings, yet I was being commanded to love those who caused me pain anyway. Luke 6:32 says, "For if ye love them which love you, what thank have ye? For sinners also love those that love them." I had to love them despite the pain of the past. That does not mean I had to be their best friend or spend time with them, it just means I had to display agape love. Displaying agape love, in this case, is when you have spiritually grown up a bit. This was difficult to accomplish. I wanted to obey His commands and not block any of my blessings by not loving them, so I had to push past my feelings and pain and receive my healing by obeying His Word.

I had suffered so much already and I had no nearby, immediate family to which I could turn. I felt like I was in a foreign land with no landing pad. I felt restricted in my current state and it was affecting everything around me. I would go to work and hate for work to come to an end because that meant I would now have to focus on my life outside of work. I would go to church and cry the entire time I was there. I felt like the woman in the Bible with the issue of blood. She had tried so many things and nothing helped. This had gone on for years and she had spent so much money trying to find a solution. I had tried everything I knew to remove the thorn in my flesh and nothing worked. It was as if nothing mattered to those around me who caused me pain. I felt like I was failing at life and had done all I knew to do to change the situation to no benefit.

Continuing to have outsiders in my life affected everything I did. I felt like I could not think. I felt numb. I felt betrayed.

I felt hopeless. I felt powerless. But just like the woman with the issue of blood, no matter how things looked and no matter how many times I tried, I would continue the journey until I met Jesus and was able to receive my healing. I had to decide that I was not going to let the pain and failures defeat me. I had to move beyond the pain, rejection, and disappointment until I had conquered the repeated thoughts in my mind of feeling unloved.

I may have felt unloved by people (and sometimes I still do) but I am always loved by God. My pain, rejection, and disappointment pushed me to become desperate to find a solution to end the madness in my life. I found the solution in Jesus and His powerful display of love for me by what He accomplished on the Cross. When He was on the Cross, He died for every one of us. Jesus had many outsiders yet He died for them all. We do not have to die a natural death for the outsiders in our lives, but we do have to die to self in order to display love for those who have hurt us. It is an art. The canvas is our mind and the battle is how the enemy plays with our minds as he tells us not to love those who have wronged us. The danger is that we walk in disobedience to the One who says we must love. The art is the emotional power to see something beyond the current state in which we find ourselves when we are experiencing pain, rejection, and disappointment.

The woman with the issue of blood in Mark 5:25-28 was made whole because she believed she could find complete healing from all that she was going through and that the answer to her pain was in Jesus. I knew I had to run to Jesus. The pain was becoming unbearable and I needed relief if I was going to survive. I was becoming emotionally and mentally drained from the pain and I was desperate for relief. I was becoming weaker in my strength and wasn't sure how I was going to see the surface of life again. When you're in the midst of painful situations, it is difficult to see anything other than the here and now. It's difficult to encourage yourself in the moment.

I wasn't sure I would be able to love again. But God spoke in 2 Corinthians 12:9 that His grace is enough for me, and my strength is made perfect in weakness. I was weak and I desperately needed His love so I could love the outsiders in return.

I was in no mood to love anybody. I hated to see anyone approach me who had hurt me. I couldn't understand why the very presence of those who had hurt me bothered me so much. I felt like I hated them for existing and being in my world. I wasn't sure how I was ever going to recover from the past. I wasn't sure I could make it through one more day with others pretending I mattered when it was clear that I did not, or I wouldn't be feeling this way.

It became increasingly more difficult to pretend that all was well with my life as my children, who lived with me, were getting older and wiser about the things that hurt me the most. I had to make some hard choices in the canvas of my life. I had to choose to love at least the agape kind of love to those who had hurt me. I don't say this proudly because I desperately wanted to be loved, but I also wanted the pain and rejection to end. I wanted to give up and walk away but I was not allowed to hate any longer because I had a greater purpose. If I lived in hate, the enemy would have caused me to abort my purpose. I finally found healing from the emotional wounds and began to walk out of the pain.

It took years and deliverance is still taking place today. At least I am not living in a state of barely existing anymore. We can move beyond our situations from scarcely existing and drowning in our emotional despair to serving and encouraging others through their valleys of despair. God has set us in strategic places and surroundings to bring hope to others. Some were able to encourage me during my difficult times but none could walk in my shoes. I had to walk through the pain and loneliness myself so I would know what it was like and could then bring deliverance to others. I found the art of loving the outsiders and I purposed for my life that I would walk in love in obedience to His Word and to receive my freedom—the freedom to no longer hate and the freedom to receive my emotional healing. Freedom to love unconditionally. Freedom to walk in purpose.

8

Sitting in His Presence Daily

I would not have been able to love the outsiders without sitting in His presence daily. There should never be a day that goes by that we are not spending quality time with God. After all, our relationship with Him is cultivated by treasured and valued time. Some might say, "But I don't have time." Then consider that the relationship you have with God is probably not valued and you are taking your relationship with Him for granted.

When we do not take the time to sit in His presence, it shows that He is just not that important to us. I believe that we make time for anything we value. I value my time with Him but sometimes life and daily schedules try to choke the life out of us, and we lose focus on what really matters. So many things in this world can become a hindrance to our relationship with God. We create more things to do for ourselves than are necessary to be able to excel in life. Our blessings are not supposed to take precedence over the One who has provided us with those blessings.

Mark 8:36 says, "What profits a man if he gains the whole world and dies and lose his soul." Pause and let this scripture sink in. Our priorities can easily be out of balance. There are several ways to regain focus and put our priorities in alignment with the Word of God so we can walk in victory and hear Him clearly. These are prayer, praise, meditation on His Word, learning to trust Him, being still and resting in His presence, and journaling. These six things took my relationship with God to an entirely different level while I was sitting in that little room created just for me and God. You may choose to use some or all of these if you like, but please make an effort to determine what will work for you.

Sitting in His presence all these years later has increased my relationship with Him. I now understand my purpose and want to walk in that purpose. Sitting in His presence will also help you find your purpose so you can change the course of your life as well as the lives of others. We are not meant to just float through life trying to accumulate wealth. We are meant to discover why we were born, then walk in that purpose. The wealth will come so that we can bless those around us who have been given to us for fulfilling the purpose. In other words, we are blessed to be a blessing, not to continuously gain and hoard wealth.

Let us consider the power of each of the six things that can bring us closer to God and bring clarity to our lives as we sit in His presence. We sit in His presence as we hunger for more of Him. We are not satisfied with the things of this world because of our need for God and His ability to love and sustain us, especially in the hard times.

Psalm 42:1 says, "As the deer panteth for the water brooks, so our soul panteth after thee oh Lord."

PRAYER

Prayer is a powerful weapon, especially when we pray the Word of God back to Him. James 5:16 says the effectual fervent prayer of the righteous man availeth much. God desires us to draw close to Him. One of the ways we can accomplish this is through prayer.

There has never been a more appropriate time to pray than at this very moment. Jesus prayed often and with fervency. He was able to bear the Cross because of His constant connection with His Father. We have the exact same access to the Father through prayer. God wants to reveal so many things to His children, but we fail to keep a line of communication open in the form of prayer. Jesus prayed with power and He knew His Father was hearing Him. I would love for us to take on the attitude that when we spend time in prayer, we pray with authority and boldness because we know the Father hears us.

Please don't pray with arrogance, but authority! Prayer is a literal conversation with God so we should act as if we know the one to whom we are speaking or praying. Prayer is a partnership with God as He has given us dominion in the Earth. Prayer is thanksgiving as we must always thank God for His mighty acts and His glorious power.

Philippians 4:6 says, "Don't be anxious or don't worry about anything, but with prayer and supplication with thanksgiving present your requests to God." Thank Him for the answers.

In my case, I eventually had to also thank Him for the problems because as I was in the fire, He was growing me. He was grooming me and stretching me. He was perfecting me and getting me ready for purpose. My purpose was found in the pain and the answer to my pain was found in the Word. We must learn to pray scripture like we've never prayed scripture before. The angels of God who move on our behalf respond to the Word of God. I know many of us think God responds to our emotional outbursts and when we are shedding countless tears or screaming in prayer during our moments of pain, but God responds to His Word. He is concerned for you and your soul because He is a loving God, but He responds to us reminding Him of the Words of life He has spoken over us. The question is, how much of His Word do we have access to already inside of us?

Spending time in the Word daily and learning scriptures helps us gain greater access to more of God's Word being planted on the inside of us. So, when trouble comes—and it will come—we have a foundation on which to stand and pray. There is purpose in prayer.

PRAISE

Praise should be who we are and what we do daily. Praise should always be on our lips. Praise should govern our path to wholeness from our brokenness. **Praise is a weapon to help us win the battle before we begin to fight.** In fact, praise comes *before* the battle.

Psalm 145:1 says, "I will exalt you, God my King, and I will praise you for ever and ever." God is great and most worthy of our praise. We express our admiration for Him when we rise in the morning. It should be one of the first things we do. When

I was alone, feeling lonely and broken, I began to sing songs of praise and immediately my countenance changed. I would walk through my situations with praise music playing and I felt such peace surrounding me.

I also want to share with you that demons had to flee and were not allowed to operate because of the praise that was being released into the atmosphere during my time of praise. In the little space that God and I shared, I had praise music playing in the background as I read His Word and meditated on the scriptures. Nothing was different about my place in life, but the atmosphere changed with praise. God inhabits the praises of His people (Psalm 22:3). He loves our praise. In fact, everything that breathes is required to praise the Lord. "Let everything that has breath praise the Lord" (Psalm 150:6).

I survived my situation not only through prayer, but through radical praise. There were days I praised God like I had lost everything—which I had, emotionally, and in some instances, physically. It allowed me to gain everything spiritually. We need to truly understand the importance of our praise. If we did, we would praise sacrificially and uninhibited. There is purpose in praise.

MEDITATION ON HIS WORD

His Word cannot fail and it will not return unto Him void but will accomplish its purposes (Isaiah 55:11). What a wonderful thought to know that God's Word has power and there is substance in His Word! We are often in need of a Word from God for our situations and sufferings. God wants us to draw close to Him and we can clearly hear what His Word has to say about every single situation we face. There is nothing new that God has not known. There are also no surprises to God about our lives. He will not be scrambling to find a solution for us when a problem arises—He has already provided a Word for us and a way of escape. The problem is, we are ignorant of His Word because we have failed to read, study, and meditate on it.

Please do not take this as some strange method of escape when I say "meditate on His Word." Joshua 1:8 says that you shall meditate on the Word of God day and night, that you will observe to do all that is written in it; for then you shall make your way prosperous and you shall have good success. This just means that you think deeply about what God is saying to you in His Word. It means that you consider what He is trying to tell you through His Word. It means that we should desire to sift the Word until we have a complete understanding of its meaning and what God really wants us to know about the scripture on which we are focusing. It doesn't have to be weird or strange, but it must be sincere and from our hearts as we meditate and allow Him to open His Word to us. We are allowing ourselves to pay attention with intensity to what God is saying. He is always speaking. Are we listening? There is purpose in meditation on God's Word.

LEARNING TO TRUST HIM

I had no hope and leaning on my own abilities was failing rapidly. I had to learn to trust God. Proverbs 3:5-6 says that we are not to lean unto our own understanding, but in all our ways we are to acknowledge Him, and He will direct our paths. Our ability to know what needs to be done in moments of crisis is minimal at best. We have no clue how to approach some of the things life throws at us, and we find ourselves struggling to know the truth and scrambling to mend the broken pieces. It is moments like these when we must learn to trust Him. We must learn to trust His Word. We must learn to trust His voice. We can only trust Him as we know His Word. Trusting in Him means that we are not depending on ourselves.

During my broken times, at first, I trusted myself because I could not trust those who promised to love me unconditionally. I placed my trust in my job and the ability to make money to sustain my family and keep balance in my life. I trusted myself to not fall apart emotionally, but to remain "together" so others could not see my failures and how everything around me was falling apart. It wasn't long before all of this began to crumble and came crashing down on me like a brick wall. I had to learn to trust God for provision and peace.

We must decide to forget about ourselves and what we can accomplish or think we can accomplish and trust that His plan for our life is better than anything we could ever imagine. We must completely surrender ourselves to God and acknowledge that His ways are higher than our ways and His thoughts are higher than our thoughts (Isaiah 55:9). This brings us to a place where we make God a priority in life. He is first and foremost in everything we do. We no longer live by our own desires but by His purpose and plan for us. We are probably not going to always like His plan. In fact, from some of my own experiences, I am confident that we will not always like His way of doing things. I wanted so many things to be different about my situations, but the fire just kept getting hotter and hotter. There were times I just knew someone had thrown me into the furnace with Shadrach, Meshach, and Abednego from the book of Daniel (chapter 3). I would fan away the flames only to have them ignite again with intensity.

Your flames may also get hot at times but stay in the fire so that you can become all that God wants you to be. Sometimes God must allow things to happen to get our attention because we need to slow down so we can hear His voice. His voice is the Holy Spirit, who is our guide through the journey of life. We often forget to acknowledge who the Holy Spirit is and what His role is in our lives. He is the third person in the Trinity, and He is sent to counsel us and guide us in all truths.

John 16:13 says that "when the Spirit of Truth is come, He will not speak of Himself, but He will speak that which He hears and will show us things to come." Therefore, we can trust that the Holy Spirit will bring us a Word from God that will show us our future as we learn to trust Him. There is purpose in learning to trust God.

BEING STILL AND RESTING IN HIS PRESENCE

God has us on His mind continuously and He cares about all the things we face in life. We should settle these thoughts in our minds and just be still and rest in His presence. God said, "Be still and know that I am God and that I will be exalted among the Heathen and I will be exalted in the Earth" (Psalm 46:10). What an amazing thought, that we just need to be still. We spend so much time wrestling with the enemy that we are often defeated, frustrated, and worn out. Just be still and rest while you wait for the enemy to be defeated, frustrated, and worn out instead. The battle has already been fought and won on your behalf. Whatever our needs are, God has already promised and met those needs.

Do you know what my needs were when I was in my moments of despair? I had financial needs. I had emotional needs. I had spiritual needs. I was lonely, in pain with sickness in my body, hospitalized from the stress, and physically and mentally exhausted. Satan had his way with me for sure. But then I came to myself and took up my fight in the spiritual realm instead of the natural realm. I took up my spiritual weapons and began to fight using the sword of the spirit. In fact, I put on the whole armor of God according to Ephesians 6:11-17. I needed to be able to stand against the fiery darts the enemy was throwing at me. I trusted God and He never faltered. I only had to obey and stand. My body and health were restored. My finances were restored. My strength was restored. God never forgot me during these times.

Today, my cup runneth over with spiritual blessings. My cup runneth over with natural and emotional healing. We should receive the overflow blessings that God promises us in Psalms 23:5. Trust Him today so that your cup overflows and you can develop purpose in allowing your overflow to flow on others who have yet to receive their deliverance. We have been equipped with the overflow not just for ourselves but for those who are yet to experience the pain and difficulty in life. For those who remain in the fire and have not yet come out as pure gold and uniquely cut diamonds, we are equipped through being still and resting in His presence. There is purpose in being still and resting in His presence.

JOURNALING

There were days when I had no words because of the pain and defeat I felt. I could barely get out of bed. I could not even pray like I should have. I was only able to groan and put my jumbled thoughts into words on a page. I began journaling when my life was falling apart to release the pressure that life had placed on me and to open the emotional and mental prison cell in which I had been caged. I could write all the things I wanted to say but was unable to formulate the words from my mouth. I found the courage to tell God my thoughts daily and I felt better. I knew that, somehow, He understood what I was trying to say to Him because I had no one else to turn to without fear of being judged.

Journaling may be an option for you as it was for me. There is no need to journal every day if the Holy Spirit is not leading you to do so, but it is therapeutic to do it often. It helps to relieve the stress brought on by our circumstances and helps us explore our feelings about what is happening in our tiny world as we fight to live and make it through the battle. We should journal to God, which will allow us to reflect on the things we discussed with God as a reference for the day when we have been delivered. Even if it doesn't feel like it now, He is going to deliver us from the pain.

Start journaling so you can release the stress and log your emotions and prayer requests for the upcoming day when God will provide the answers to those prayers. There is purpose in journaling.

9

***

Honoring the Holy One and His Anointing

SITTING in His presence daily leads us to a life of holiness. Okay, there's that word "holiness" again. We have such a negative view of the word "holy" because of how many of us were taught based on our religious backgrounds. For some of us, it's not understood at all or we have a mental picture of people who look or dress a certain way. Let me ask you to focus on the word holy from a different and true perspective.

1 Peter 1:16 tells us to be holy because He is Holy. God is calling us to a higher level in Him. He wants us to land on a different playing field where we are always winners.

Consider the word holy for a moment and think of other words that come to mind. Ponder what God meant when He commanded us to be holy. He wants us to live life a certain way so that He can draw others into the Kingdom of God through us. We must be willing to allow all things to work for His purpose and plan.

During my periods of despair, I had the choice to be bitter and angry or not. At first, I was angered by how people caused another person so much pain. To move on from this low point in my life, I had to make a choice. That choice was for me and no one else. I chose to be a representative of the Kingdom. It wasn't easy at first but it became easier the closer I got to the Holy One and received His Anointing. I was not, nor am I today, strong enough to overlook someone else's faults, especially when I'm on the receiving end of the emotional rollercoaster. At times, I would say to myself, *I can be strong and be the one to act like the Christian here.* Then other times I would say, *Why should I be the one to forgive and show the love of Christ? Why should I be the one who is forgiving and loving?*

I had to walk in the Anointing of the Holy One. I wanted His presence in my life. I must be honest and say I wanted to play the game well and not allow my hurt to show so the enemy didn't feel he had won. I wasn't going to give up my joy that easily. My happiness was already gone but I was definitely keeping my joy.

At the beginning of my tumultuous relationships with the outsiders, when things were not going well, I would contemplate ways to get even. I was hurting so the ones hurting me needed to hurt as well. I spent so much energy trying to make their lives miserable that I only made things worse.

We are not meant to get even but rather to show mercy toward each other. This isn't an easy thing to do and I am not saying that I was a better Christian than anyone else because only God can be the judge of that. I am simply saying that as spiritual revelation is gained, we should use the things God has taught us to not only make life better for ourselves, but for those who are living in ignorance of His Word.

I always asked those who treated me badly, how would they feel if I was treating them that way? There were often no words or answers to this question. So, I had no other choice but to pick up the pieces and move on with my life. It became important that I learned the lessons of life through the pain and silence of others who offered no answers to what I considered very important questions. I needed the answers to feel like I mattered. I needed the answers because I thought that if they answered, there might be some consideration for what I was feeling for a moment.

But that moment never came. I was left all alone in a world that had been created for me. It was a silent world that I did not ask for or care to have. I just wanted my old life back, even if it wasn't perfect. At least it was better than the nightmare I was currently living. However, just like any nightmare, we eventually wake up and realize that it is over. We realize that we do not have to be afraid anymore. We realize that we're loved and protected from the danger found in the horrendous thoughts and feelings that had us locked into the nightmare in the first place. We realize that we are His and that we have landed in the arms of the Holy One. What an amazing place to be! We are safe in the arms of the Holy One and His Anointing.

Have you considered who the Holy One is and why it is termed this way? The Holy One is our Father, who is in the midst of all the storms and nightmares. He is Holy and He requires holiness from us. Holiness is a lifestyle that becomes a part of who we are, and we are to walk in holiness daily. We cannot choose to put on holiness when we feel like we need to. Holiness is us walking by faith in His authority. We surrender everything about us to Him and He takes up the reins of our lives and guides us. We become totally dependent on Him for everything and every answer.

I had no answers to any of life's problems. I did not have any answers to this tumultuous life I found myself in, for sure. I had to surrender everything over to Him. In my surrendering, I found the Holy One and with Him came His Anointing. He attempted to guide me through the rough spaces, but I hadn't let go yet. And I had to let go so He could guide me.

I depended on His Anointing to take me through paths that felt foreign to me. In my journey through the rough spaces, I found myself becoming more like Him. I began to take on His nature. I adopted His character and traded in my own because His ways and thoughts were so much higher than my own. I found myself walking in His Anointing. His Anointing was—at that time, and still is today—very refreshing.

In I John 2:27, the Anointing which we have received of Him abides in us, and we do not need that any man to teach us. The same Anointing teaches us all things, and is truth and no lie, and even as the Anointing has taught us, we shall stand and abide in Him.

The Anointing taught me so many things during the hard times and during the storms when things were foggy and unclear. He spoke to me when things didn't make sense. I had so much trouble focusing on every moment and just to be able to put one foot in front of the other was a chore. I needed His wisdom and guidance and the Anointing of God provided that roadmap. It allowed me to have an escape route so I could survive when the highways in life were too crowded with emotions and reactions to the moment.

The presence of God afforded me the gift of peace so I could function in everyday life. There was no time to give up. I had to keep pushing to rise to the top again. God had anointed and gifted me to be greater than my circumstances and I needed to embrace His presence. I needed to consider things and people beyond myself. I needed to consider my children and their strong dependence on me. I needed to teach them about the Anointed One and His Anointing. I needed them to have staying power, to have an option if they needed to fight someday.

I pray that I have taught them to fight the battles of life in the presence of God. I pray they have developed a lifestyle of holiness. And I pray that you have or will also develop a lifestyle of holiness. It is through a lifestyle of holiness that we can discover our purpose for the pain and live solely for our Heavenly Father.

Begin to reflect on how you see yourself and where you would like to be as a person who represents holiness. Try to conquer the pain and walk in your purpose by living a true life of holiness as you are filled with His presence. It may be difficult at first because sometimes it's hard to let go of the pain of the past. We must depend on the Anointing of God to take us where we want to go in life as the Anointing is the Holy Spirit that leads and guides us into all truth. He is the only one who can help rescue us from our fractured and broken pasts and help us put our futures back together again. He can sever us from our painful past and give us a future of hope.

The good news is that the Anointing isn't just for some of us, it is for all of us who confess Christ as our Lord and Savior. **This Anointing of the Holy Spirit allows us to love when we would otherwise hate.** I felt I had lots of reasons to hate but I chose not to walk the path of hate. I chose to walk in the

Anointing. I chose life. I chose to walk out of the emotional prison cell and make a difference for the Kingdom of God because He has anointed me.

Isaiah 61:1-3 (NIV) says, "The Spirit of the Sovereign Lord is upon me and He has anointed me to proclaim good news to the poor. He has sent me to bind up the broken hearted, to proclaim freedom for the captives, and release the prisoners from darkness. To proclaim the year of the Lord's favor and the day of vengeance of our God. To comfort all who mourn and provide for those who grieve in Zion. To bestow on them a crown of beauty instead of ashes, the oil of joy instead of mourning and a garment of praise instead of a spirit of despair. They will be call oaks of righteous, a planting of the Lord for the display of His splendor."

I encourage all of us to step outside of our emotional prison walls once we have been anointed and have been given the keys to deliver others. We have been anointed to set others free. We have been anointed to restore others to Christ. We have been anointed to bring healing. We have been anointed to proclaim the gospel to set captives free and release those who are bound.

We must honor the Holy One with our lives. Choose freedom. Choose new life. Choose to be used by Him to be a blessing to others. Choose to be holy and walk in holiness. Choose purpose.

10

Becoming a Blessing to
Those Around You

WALKING in holiness is a lifestyle while choosing to be a blessing is a heart issue. We choose to bless others because we care and because it is what our Heavenly Father desires of us because it pleases Him. We take on the role of a servant as we become a blessing to those around us. Are we offended when others consider us a servant? Many of us like to sit in kingly places and on priestly seats. We like all the attention and bells and whistles when we enter a room. We make life all about us. The idea of a servant doesn't quite cut it for us. Yet the Bible clearly says that he that is greatest among you shall be the servant (Matthew 23:11).

Taking on the role of a servant has its rewards and benefits. It places us in a position where we can bless others instead of always blessing ourselves. Consider for a moment the woman in Matthew 20:21-22, who asked Jesus to allow her sons to sit on His right and left in the Kingdom. Jesus had to say to her, "You don't know what you are asking of me because will your sons be able to drink of the same cup and be baptized with the same baptism?"

Jesus came to serve, not to be served. Even though their answers were yes, they were seeking status. We must use our purpose and learn to serve. As God is propelling us into our already ordained purpose, He is asking us to serve others. I had to walk countless women through their pain many times while I was still walking through some of my most painful moments.

For example, you may be led, as I was led, to accept a particular job. Your places of employment are meant to be an assignment from our Heavenly Father. We never know why He places us in strategic positions in the marketplace. Have you ever considered that there may be someone there who needs the things God has placed in you? There are people in various places waiting on your purpose. Therefore, God plants us in places to serve others and to bring Him glory. What about that person working on your job who barely speaks to others and seems to be angry all the time? Have you met anyone on your job that fits this description? You may even feel as if they disappear and leave you to do all the work. You do not need to pry into their life or gossip to others about the behavior of that person. You simply need to allow God's love to shine through you every day.

You should speak and smile every morning, even when you have issues that are bringing you to a low point in your life. I have been at the crossroads of life and have still been able to smile and move forward as a representative of the Kingdom of God. I have also been at the place where I needed a representative of the Kingdom of God to show me some grace. I was devoid of the funds I needed to pay my bills and make it to the end of the month. I was driving a borrowed car to work and wasn't sure how I was going to afford another one on my own. I had plenty of reasons to be angry and miserable. But I chose Jesus and along with Him came joy. One day, that person on the job may engage in a meaningful conversation with you about their life and what is happening. They may begin to cleave to you, and you may realize that the one they are truly drawn to was Jesus and the anointing of God.

We have nothing to offer within our own power. **Only the power of God draws others into the space we are in.** He draws them to Himself through our obedience to being in purpose. We simply need to lift Him up with our lives. As time goes on, others may speak more about where they are in life and their lives will begin to unfold so that we can provide them with answers to their situations. We must walk the path with others even though we may be experiencing the same or worse issues. The key is to never have a pity party and talk about how bad our own situations are, but to try to bring some light and hope into the other person's struggles. By doing this, we heal while bringing healing to others.

I once was tasked with the assignment of comforting someone who had a marriage that was falling apart. It just so happened that at the time, my own life was falling apart too but I did not talk about my troubles. In fact, if anyone asked me, my response was always, "All is well." So, I simply asked the person I was comforting to fight for the marriage. I asked them to fight for the freedom of their spouse and to understand that their spouse needed them. The marriage was not one of adultery but certainly had many emotional wounds. Even so, their fight to save the marriage was completely transformable. There was no desire to walk away from the marriage. They both wanted to have a whole family again. What they both were feeling and receiving were just lies from the enemy.

Do not get me wrong, the things they were experiencing were real and valid. The experience was very painful for them to walk through. They were being shaken and tested beyond any natural abilities. The pain that each was experiencing was deeply rooted pain that had been occurring for years. My purpose was to hold up their arms as they made their way through the battle. My purpose for meeting them was to help them with the tears that were being shed and the pain that was their everyday story in life. My purpose was to encourage them to go one more mile when I am sure they felt like ending the race. My purpose was fulfilled as their marriage relationship was restored. They needed support from another person who believed in God and His power to resurrect dead things. They needed to know that Jesus cared. Not only was their marriage restored, but they also developed a relationship with the Holy One and His Anointing. That was the greatest fulfillment of all as they came to know God and find emotional and spiritual freedom.

Someone needs your support to help them progress on their journey. As we look for answers in the madness of life, we are to seek out others. As believers and followers of Christ, we are to provide this support and be diligent in our privilege to serve others who are in need. I find it a blessing to my own life when I begin to bless others. I find it purposeful and fulfilling. I find it pure joy.

Blessing others can be very rewarding but that should not be our motive. We should bless others because Philippians 2:3-4 states that we are to "let nothing be done through strife and vainglory, but we are to esteem others better than ourselves." We are not to look to our own things, but to the things of others. This does not mean that we do not care about our own needs, but God asked us to water others and we shall be watered in return. We do not need to be concerned because God will meet every need we have if we would just take the focus off ourselves.

The Bible says in Matthew 6 that we are to "take no thought for our lives" as He cares for us and meets all our needs. I had the perfect opportunity to say to the couple I ministered to that I understood what they were going through. I could have encouraged them to just let go of the relationship and walk away. In fact, they had already let go to a degree. She had moved out of her home and left her spouse. She considered that part of her life to be over. She had reached a point where she thought there was no return. By watching their actions, I saw that the move out of the home was obviously causing both of them great pain and distress. Yet, God restored it all and the enemy lost the battle.

I encouraged them to honor God by honoring His Word. I invited them to church, but more importantly, I invited them to know God and to accept the things Jesus had done for them. I encouraged them to develop a closer relationship with the Father so they could receive their healing. I chose to give to them the gift of life in Jesus when I needed more myself. I needed many natural blessings, but I had spiritual blessings I was able to give away and which God replenished daily.

There are also benefits in blessing as the Bible says that those who bless others are abundantly blessed and those who help others will be helped (Proverbs 11:25). I was never lacking anything because as I was pouring out my life, God was constantly filling me up again. It wasn't long before my cup was running over with both natural and spiritual blessings. I wanted to pour out more. I wanted others to be whole. I wanted others to know God the way I knew Him. I wanted others to experience inexplicable joy. I wanted others to discover the ability to be a blessing, and what a privilege and how rewarding being a blessing can be.

We should seek more avenues to be a blessing to others and we should begin in our homes with the ones who are closest to us. We are often accused of being more kind to those who are on the outside than the ones we live with daily. We spend more of our waking hours in a world that cares little about us than we do most of the time with our families, especially if we have jobs. We allow the world to devour us until we have nothing left when we arrive home at the end of the day. Our spouses and children are rightfully waiting for their due share of us. God created the family unit as the foundation, yet we are being torn apart by the enemy because we are just trying to survive in this fallen world.

In Genesis 1:27-28, we find where God created the first family. He provided everything the family would need before ever creating man. Satan desires to destroy the family. I fought so hard for my privilege to have a family because I understood this truth. The love between a husband and wife and the sanctity of marriage allow us to see how Christ loves the church. The Bible says for husbands to love their wives even as Christ also loved the church and gave himself for it (Ephesians 5:25). The family is God's way of saying we are to value relationships. We should be a blessing to those with whom we live or are close to us. God has created our homes as safe places as we lean on and provide pleasure and comfort to each other. After caring for our homes, then we care for others.

We should seek to be a blessing to those who are on our jobs or in the marketplace. We never know where a person's life has taken them. We never know what battle another person is fighting. Just because people don't tell us when they are experiencing difficult times doesn't mean they are in a good place in life. We must allow our lives to reflect Christ. When we allow our lives to reflect Christ, we can bless others and make a difference. We want to help others walk through their painful moments. We want them to feel like they matter—because they *do* matter. We all do. Even those in our neighborhoods matter. We must represent the love of Christ well in our neighborhoods. We may be the only God they ever see prior to developing a relationship with Jesus Christ.

The Bible says we are letters known and read by everyone. Let us be kind to our neighbors so we can win them to Christ if need be. Let us be a blessing because it is commanded by God and obedience to God is the righteous thing to do. Most of all, let us be a blessing because others need it and we introduce Christ without ever wearing the outward Christian regalia. We wear it from within. It ties us to our purpose to save and seek those who are lost.

We are to serve and minister to others and do it cheerfully. In doing so, Hebrews 6:10 says, "God is not unrighteous to forget your work and labor of love, which ye have shown toward His name, in that ye have ministered to the saints, and do minister."

Be a living epistle. Be a blessing. Be a servant. Be a person of purpose.

God already claimed you as his own and saw the great woman of purpose you would someday be!

11

Walking in Purpose

WHAT is the purpose for which God created each of us? The answer to this question might lie in the current life you are living as you may have already found purpose in life. Or it may be events from your past that have caused you to want to make a difference. Whatever we think the answer to this question may be, it is not up to us to design purpose for our lives. God has already determined purpose for us. Everything we have faced in life, every road we have traveled, every painful moment we have been through, has been orchestrated to bring us to a place where we can make a difference in the life of another person.

We are our sisters' and brothers' keepers. We are to let the situations we face cause growth in each of us so that we can water and fertilize another person and foster their growth. This is not to say that we will be able to cultivate everyone we encounter because we are not meant to water and fertilize everyone, but God has determined those we are to journey through life with so they can grow and live by what we have to offer them. If we ask God for revelation and have a willing heart, those we are meant to cultivate will cross our paths at some point in time. We must be cognizant of how we approach others and how we present ourselves daily because we never know when that person will receive—both directly and indirectly—what we have been purposed to do. Someone is always watching our lives whether we realize it or not. So, as we ponder how we are going to present ourselves, let me help with the understanding of purpose.

Purpose is the reason for which we have been created or for which we exist. Let me ask you...did we just happen to end up here on Earth? Did God have a plan for allowing us to be born in this time and this generation (whatever generation we were born into)? We are here because we are world-changers. We have the power of the Holy Spirit inside of us to make a difference in the lives of others.

We must discover the tools that have been given to us to change the world. Our worlds will look different depending on our sphere of influence. This means that no matter where God has us every day—whether in an office, factory, outside, or in our homes—we are to represent His character in order to make a difference and change the world. There is so much work to be done. I would like for us to stop looking at someone else's works and contributions and envying what they are doing. It's OUT OF ORDER! It's out of God's order for your life! The price another woman of God paid to gain her purpose is far more than any of us could probably handle had we endured the same. If each one of us had the opportunity to share our stories or provide our testimonies, just as I have shared bits and pieces of mine, we would be blown away and amazed by what others have endured and are currently enduring. God, just give me my own cross to bear as I am sure I would not be able to bear a cross meant for others.

Use the life God has given you to change the life of another person. Do not be silent any longer, as God will lead you to another who needs to hear your story. Whether your story involves the things I mentioned at the beginning of this book or is something totally different, we are the bridge to another person's freedom as we stand in the gap, having conquered the issues in our lives.

Some of us will share on a widescreen with the world. Some will meet the needs of others through purpose in our small surroundings or on a much smaller screen. Let me share a story about two women of the Bible who had major purpose in life. One was on a small screen while the other was very well known, yet both carried a significant purpose and I am sure this is why they were created.

A prophetess named Anna was intentioned by God to intercede in the coming of the Messiah, and she was graced to pray and fast in the temple toward this end (Luke 2:36-38). What an amazing purpose! She was called to pray and intercede on behalf of the coming King who would be the Savior of the world.

Many of us are called to pray for others even if we never have a conversation with them. God has gifted some of us to be true intercessors and to fervently pray on behalf of others for things that concern Him. God will begin to show those who are gifted and willing to pray about things to come and entrust them with matters that are near and dear to His heart.

I want to share an experience with you about how God entrusts me to pray for others I have never met. Sometimes He just gives me a name in the middle of the night. There was a time that my spirit being spent the night in another country in the home of a family who was about to be attacked by the enemy. I can still see the family vividly and I would recognize the mother at this very moment if I saw her. The mother of the family was pregnant and the enemy was coming for her child. I lay in the foyer while the family slept and prayed in the natural and the Spirit for protection over the household. I watched the enemy leave the grounds of that home and I knew immediately that all was well.

Can God trust you to pray? Can He trust that when others have turmoil in their lives, and we are aware, that we will fall before the King and pour out our hearts as we would for our own family and loved ones? Can we stand in the gap for another even when we are tired and don't feel like praying? Could it be that you have the Anna spirit for the gift of prayer? Even though Anna may not have been well known by many, her purpose was significant. When we consider her life, some of us might relate to her.

Anna was married and lost her husband at a young age. She was only married for seven years but was a widow for over eighty years and spent most of those years behind the scenes in the temple praying with the expectancy of Jesus. I suspect that many of us have purposes that are behind the scenes and we neglect to walk in our purpose or purposes because no one will know or we will not be recognized. Guess what? The One who matters the most notices that we are not welcoming what He is asking us to do. Who are we really aiming to please, man or our Heavenly Father?

Now let us consider a more well-known prophetess. Her

name was Deborah. Deborah was a prophetess-warrior-judge and the only female warrior-judge of the Old Testament. This was before the Kingdoms were formed in Israel.

Deborah was a prophetess and the wife of Lapidoth, judged Israel at that time. She used to sit under the palm of Deborah between Ramah and Bethel in the hill country of Ephraim; and the people of Israel came up to her for judgment (Judges 4:4-5).

During her time, she accompanied an army into battle and explained to her general, that she would surely go with him; nevertheless, the road on which they are going would not lead to his glory (Judges 4:9). Deborah was wise and she availed herself to walk in purpose as she was most certainly a woman of purpose. I suspect that she was respected because of her dependence on God's guidance. I also realize that Deborah was probably a woman before her time as she was the only female judge of her time. In fact, as she led the army as a warrior, she told Barak that she would accompany him but that he needed to be aware that the war would be won at the hand of a woman.

Wow! What purpose and power we have as women! We are to understand that God has created us to do amazing and out-of-the-box things. We must be willing to say yes to His will and purpose for our lives no matter where the journey takes us. It will take us through some of the darkest valleys and some of the lowest points in life, only to have us soar above the mountains in the end. Deborah had to endure to walk in purpose because she was also a wife in addition to being a warrior and judge. Many of us understand the honor of being a wife but only some of us understand having the office of warrior or military leadership or being a judge and walking in the place of conducting disputes among the people.

Some of us are Annas or Deborahs. Many of us have given birth to children and they also have a great purpose. The enemy attacks us and our children so that we cannot walk in purpose and greatness. May I suggest that we fight for our purpose and do not allow the enemy to abort our purpose in life, since God has already designed a job for each of us to do? Since He has given us purpose, we must desire to fulfill that purpose. We can fulfill our purpose by discovering, developing, and implementing the purpose or purposes for which we have been created.

Discovering your purpose is the first step to walking in purpose. First, remember it has never been our job to create our purpose. It is simply our role to discover why He created us.

How do we discover our purpose? Pray and use your trials and what keeps you up at night. What keeps tugging at you to make a difference? Matthew 13:44-46 says, "The kingdom of heaven is like unto treasure hid in a field; which when a man hath found, he hideth, and for joy thereof goeth and selleth all that he hath, and buyeth that field. Again, the kingdom of heaven is like unto a merchant man, seeking goodly pearls: Who, when he had found one pearl of great price, went and sold all that he had, and bought it."

When we discover purpose, we give our all because from that purpose and making a difference in someone else's life, we get joy. It truly is better to give than to receive. We already have planted on the inside of us the seeds to produce increase, we just have to discover the type of seeds we have. Please don't try to cultivate roses if you have daisy seeds. There are different types of plant food, different water requirements, and different amounts of sunlight needed for each type of seed.

Discovering your purpose is a divine assignment. Lord, please reveal your clear assignment for our lives. Help us walk in the calling and purpose for which you have assigned us.

We are only gifted and anointed for the purpose for which

He has assigned us. I am not sure how I got to the purpose of women other than walking through my own pain and disappointment. I made it to the other side, so I can tell others how to make it out of their seasons of pain and at the very least, how to endure the fire until God delivers them from the pain. It is my purpose to walk with them during the journey to ensure that they can stand. It is my purpose that the people God has purposed me to meet have a shoulder to cry on and a hand to hold as they walk through the fire. Therefore, it leads me to develop my purpose.

Developing purpose often stems from pain. Your pain is a part of the development stage or process. We are repeatedly trying to get out of the fire, and we are just being refined. Yes, the fire gets hot and the pain feels unbearable. Nevertheless, God has a plan. Think about the olive tree, before it can be used to bring forth olives and olive oil. The more virgin the oil, the greater the price will be for the oil.

We are priceless women of God. We have value and worth that make us unique and special. I recently discovered that silver is refined in the fire seven times before it is completed for use. Think also about gold and diamonds and the process from the mines to the markets, how they're refined in the fire several times before the gem comes forth. For gold and silver, fire is the best way to purify. When all the impurities are gone from gold, you have 24-karat gold—the most valuable grade.

Consider yourself 24-karat gold in the eyes of God. Zechariah 13:9 (NLT) says, "I will bring that group through the fire and make them pure. I will refine them like silver and purify them like gold. They will call on my name, and I will answer them. I will say, 'These are my people,' and they will say, 'The LORD is our God.'"

For diamonds, there's blasting, digging, cutting, sawing,

and polishing. The longer the gem is in the fire, the clearer it becomes. God has got to do some cutting on us and it's sometimes painful. Stay in the fire so you can implement the purpose. In most cases, no matter how much we want to get out of the fire, we can't until it is time.

Implementing our gifts brings glory to God for the purpose for which He has made us. Many use their gifts and callings to serve and magnify themselves; others use their gifts to serve Satan, often without realizing that Satan is receiving the glory due God. Think about someone who can sing. Without the anointing of God, it is just a gift. Our purposes must always be in pursuit of the will of God. Many souls will never know the love of Christ because we refuse to walk in purpose and use the gifts God has equipped us with to fulfill that purpose.

So, let's ask ourselves, are we making an impact for the Kingdom of God through our purpose? It is our responsibility to *discover* and *implement* our purpose, but it is God's responsibility to *create* the purpose. We can do none of this without the Holy Spirit. We will give an account of what we did with the gifts He gave us. Job 42:2 (NKJV) says, "I know that you can do everything, and that no purpose of yours can be withheld from you."

So, walk in purpose. Walk in love. Walk in anticipation of who God has created you to be. Walk in His will for your life so you can deliver others. He has designed us for greatness upon the Earth as we occupy it until He comes again.

12

Designed for Destiny

OUR initial purpose is to be disciples of Jesus Christ and become disciple-makers. We must always keep this as our primary focus and purpose. However, God has created us for more, not that anything is greater. Your purpose often leads others to Christ when you bring healing into their lives. I knew I was designed for something other than walking in grief when I was able to assist others in walking the path I had yet to conquer myself. I began walking through the pain with others as I went through my own pain. Walking with others gave me the peace of knowing that I was making another person feel better even when I felt miserable.

Maybe I should share a few things about my humble

beginnings in life as I bring the book to a close. It may help you understand who I am a bit more.

I was raised as a farm girl in a small township. As a child, around the age of six, I would sometimes find a tree for shade and lie at the end of the garden in the afternoon. I would gaze up at the heavens and say, "I wonder why I'm here? Who am I?" I could lie there for minutes to hours just thinking about how I ended up on Earth and why. I would sometimes fall asleep in the garden just dreaming about life and the family God had blessed me with. I had wonderful parents and seven siblings, and we loved each other.

I remember us sharing meals and how much that meant. I remember sharing moments of laughter and fun while playing games and telling stories. I remember working very hard as a family to make life fulfilling and to be able to eat every day. Needless to say, we worked hard as farmers and cultivators. I don't ever remember dreaming about being a wife or a mother at any time or what that would be like. I guess that's the independent part of me.

I do remember going to church and sitting on a pew from the age of six to about eight years old, and coming home often and preaching the entire sermon on Sunday afternoon to anything and anyone who would listen, including dolls and the dogs. My mother would sit on the porch and I am sure she was listening. My brothers often laughed at me because I preached even back then. They weren't laughing because I was preaching; they were laughing because I was preaching to objects and things as opposed to people.

God was giving me a voice even then. At eight years old, I was baptized in the outdoor pool at the Baptist Church one Saturday morning after a week of revival. I decided on my own to be baptized with the prompting of the Holy Spirit, even at the age of eight. I would often sit in a selected spot on my own, not necessarily near my immediate family or my mom, while at church. On the Sunday I decided it was time for me to walk down the aisle and "join the church," I remember an elderly lady trying to get me to sit down. I politely pushed past her to get to the front of the church so I could confess Jesus and be baptized. Even as I write this account, I have tears in my eyes because I remember that moment and what it felt like as if it were yesterday. I wanted to know Jesus so desperately that I knew I had to take that next step.

Now, this is not to say that I had a perfect life or never went astray as I grew up. I have made many mistakes and never once did I not feel God tugging at my heart to "get it right" during those times. I am thankful He never left me alone. I am thankful for His conviction because even during those times, He let me know He loved me and wanted to restore me.

My journey continued through my teenage years with a few things that were displeasing to God, but mostly I stayed as close as possible to the Word of God I had received until the end of my high school years. Then, it all started as I became an adult.

I never struggled to be accepted until I became older and began to experience life on a different level as an adult. Going away to college brought a whole new set of challenges that I had not been exposed to before that time and for which I was unprepared. I had more freedom and a choice to do the right thing. I will say that I was determined I would do nothing to make my mother hang her head or be ashamed of. I never stopped going to church. I found a church to attend the very next Sunday after arriving on the college campus. I was four hours away from home and without a car, so I either went to the campus chapel or a nearby church that sent a van to pick up students who wanted to attend.

I attended every Sunday even if there was no one else attending with me. I needed Jesus even then, and this need continued throughout my life as a foundation for what I would face later on. Then I entered an adult relationship with another Christian who had also professed Christ. I will admit, he taught me a few things, especially about forgiveness. Thankfully so, since I would need that bit of advice later in life just trying to row through the stormy waters of life to keep from drowning. Yet, I am so grateful as life has brought me both beauty and pain, which propelled me to purpose. My children have brought me such joy and honestly, may have played a huge part in why I was able to push through the chaos while waiting for God to bring order to my life. I stayed a long time in some of my toxic relationships, wondering about life once again and why I was in that situation, and why God was taking so long to "fix" the problematic people in my life.

I must smile here because God was fixing the problematic me. That's not to say others didn't need fixing, it was just not my job to fix them. They belong to the Creator just like I do. The Creator is the only one who can fix His creation since we are designed and instrumentally and strategically placed here on Earth by Him.

I needed fixing. My growth in Him had grown stale from when I was that eight-year-old who just had to make my way to the front of the church and profess my love for Him, and how much I knew Jesus was the Son of God and that He had died for me.

Going through the many seasons of life from the age of eight, making it through my twenties and thirties, and even now, I can say that many lessons were learned and I definitely grew up a lot. I unquestionably discovered purpose. For this, I am thankful as I take this journey with others. It has been a long time since I was the six-year-old lying in the garden trying to figure out who I was and questioning God about my identity. Through my journey in life, I have discovered my purpose for being here and those questions are sufficiently answered.

Now, consider your background and the things that have impacted you the most in life. Furthermore, consider what would be the "one thing" you are most concerned about that keeps you up at night or constantly churns in your spirit—the thing you would do without pay if you had the opportunity. The one thing that keeps me up at night is knowing that people are hurting. Knowing that others are crying with broken hearts and broken dreams gives me direction and purpose.

God gives us a heart of love for those around us and we must act upon the things we are feeling. It may not be a feeling of not being loved—it might be a single mother or father who is struggling to feed and clothe their children. It might be widows who have too much time alone and need a little bit of company from time to time. Whatever is on your heart that lines up with the Word of God, consider that it may be purpose.

There was a time when it was just me and my children, and most of the time, we did not have enough money for the month. However, when we did have a bit of extra, I found other struggling single mothers and fathers I had befriended and took their children for the day so they could have a bit of time for themselves. God honors our efforts but we must be willing to make the effort.

As I close this purposeful work, it might be helpful for you to identify one person in the Bible that may be of interest to you or resembles the "one thing" you can envision yourself doing. Study this passage of scripture as you ask God about your assigned purpose or purposes. You can be used by God to bring change through your gifts. **God has called you with purpose and He wants you to fulfill that purpose.**

Romans 8:30 states, "Moreover whom he did predestinate, them he also called: and whom he called, them he also justified: and whom he justified, them he also glorified."

We have such awesome reasons for being on this Earth and it is not just to take up space. We are here to effect change and to create better for others as God creates better for us. So, if you are that person who has suffered infant or pregnancy loss, infertility, or the death of a loved one who was closer to you than anyone can imagine, and are dealing with the grief left by the holes in your heart; if you are dealing with health issues where you had to fight for your life, divorce and infidelity, and wayward children who have lost their way in life, you are equipped to help others who find themselves attempting to make their way out of the valleys from the pain their issues may have caused.

I cannot effectively help someone who may have suffered infant or pregnancy loss if I have never walked that path in life. I also cannot effectively help those who have wayward children who have lost their way. But I can walk the road with others who have suffered pain from the loss of loved ones, health-related issues, and those feeling unloved, rejected, and who are suffering from broken hearts. Just as I can help them walk these paths, you have the ability to help others walk a different path. You will find joy and fulfillment in doing so.

We are meant to serve others and be a blessing to those around us. The most miserable people on Earth are those who are self-serving and constantly focus on themselves. We are created to be more than self-servers. We are created to serve others. The Father sees us as valuable and competent enough to walk in the purpose He has given us when we seek to help others. As we are called to serve others, we are solely dependent on the Holy Spirit to lead and guide us in the purpose for which He has called us.

In order to walk in His purpose for our lives, we are to walk in His Word daily as He orders our footsteps. He created our lives to bring healing and peace to others through our purpose. No matter our past, our future is with Him and the purpose He has given to each of us.

Discover your purpose and walk in your purpose wholeheartedly. A woman of purpose understands that she centers her every move on living her purpose once she discovers it. Nothing can cause her to retreat to a place where she will not be used by God. Her purpose will always be the center of her joy. Therefore, walk in your purpose with boldness while making an impact for the Kingdom of God!

CPSIA information can be obtained
at www.ICGtesting.com
Printed in the USA
LVHW050810060620
657560LV00003B/898

9 781973 690566